Dinosaurs

John Man

Exeter Books

NEW YORK

A Bison Book

Contents

PAGE 1: A mid-nineteenth century restoration of pterosaurs that shows them as hairy and bat-like. Pterosaurs were, however, once classified as reptiles and the possibility that any reptile could have hair was generally discounted. Now it is known that Pterosaurs were hairy, and the reptilian classification seems strange. PREVIOUS PAGES: A painting of a prehistoric scene. LEFT: A Brachiosaurus skeleton that was unearthed at Tendaguru, Tanzania and now stands in the East Berlin Natural History Museum. It was the heaviest (80–100 tons) and the tallest (40 feet) of all land animals. It owed its great strength in part to the fact that its front legs were, uniquely, longer than its back legs.

First published in USA
By Exeter Books
Distributed by Bookthrift
Exeter is a trademark of Bookthrift Marketing, Inc.
Bookthrift is a registere
trademark of Bookthrift Marketing, Inc.
New York, New York.

ISBN 0–671–06145–3

Printed in Hong Kong.

Reprinted 1986

Introduction

Every child knows about dinosaurs. Countless six-year-olds across the Western World can identify a picture of a *Brontosaurus*, *Stegosaurus* or *Tyrannosaurus*. The complexity of the names does not bother them. They take as much pleasure in the names as in the power of the creatures themselves. Their knowledge often strikes their parents as precocious.

But that is usually as far as it gets. About this subject, parents seldom know much more than their children. Most people acquire little more than an attitude toward the creatures—an image of huge cumbersome brutes, sometimes

The 70-foot, 30-ton Apatosaurus *(which used to be called* Brontosaurus*) is, in the words of one scientist, 'literally Mr Dinosaur himself' for the public at large.*

fierce, perhaps weighed down with armor, certainly stupid, heading toward inevitable extinction, displaced by the agile, intelligent, adaptable mammals that led to man.

The plain fact is that dinosaurs need a new deal. Their image does them little justice and beliefs about them are all too often just plain wrong.

For one thing, the dinosaurs were all extinct some 60 million years before even the most primitive man made his appearance on the earth. Man's fossil record extends back perhaps four million years. The dinosaurs, when they became extinct, had been on the earth for about 140 million years. Only after they vanished did the mammals get their chance. The dinosaurs and their related groups of reptiles thus dominated the earth for at least twice as long as the mammals have been around. The mammals as a whole—let alone our own species, *Homo sapiens*—will have to last another 80 million years to qualify as an equal success.

Moreover, the dinosaurs dominated the land as the mammals do now and they were as varied in their life styles as the mammals are.

Many hundreds of tons of dinosaur fossils have revealed that there were several hundred species, ranging from creatures not much bigger than chickens up to the more familiar 80-ton giants. Indeed, because the dinosaurs can be known only from their fossil record—the scattered remnants that by some rare coincidence became trapped in the right sort of sediments and turned to stone—there must be scores of other species yet to be discovered. There must also be scores more, no parts of which were fossilized; of these we shall never know anything.

Slow? Cumbersome? Ill-equipped for survival? No indeed. Many species were adapted for rapid and sustained action on their hind legs. Even the giants were beautifully engineered to cope with their massive bulk on dry land. Some recent reconstructions of *Diplodocus*,

In Walt Disney's Fantasia, *the dinosaurs lumber to their death under a pitiless desert sun, perishing in a fruitless search for vanishing water holes. In fact, the climate at the end of the Age of Reptiles became cooler, not hotter.*

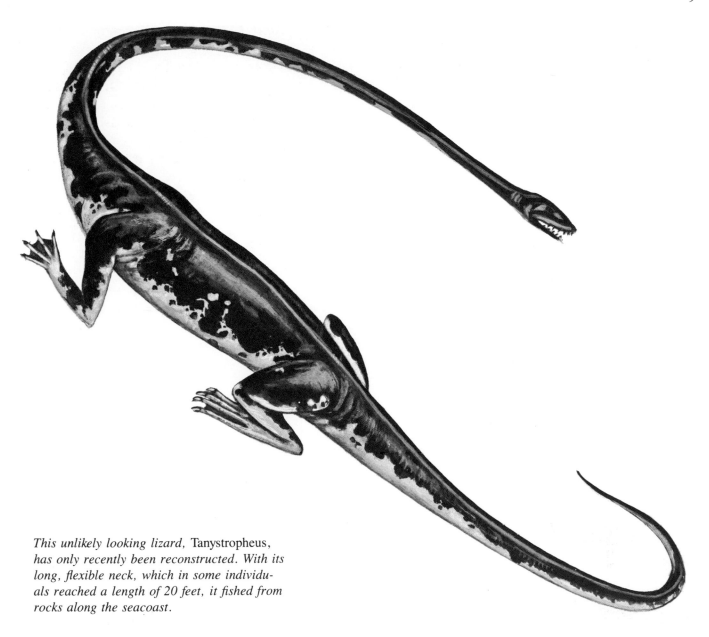

This unlikely looking lizard, Tanystropheus, *has only recently been reconstructed. With its long, flexible neck, which in some individuals reached a length of 20 feet, it fished from rocks along the seacoast.*

the largest of the dinosaurs at almost 90 feet, show it as quite capable of galloping giraffe-like across the ancient plains.

Recent research is rewriting the dinosaur story. One major issue is: were the dinosaurs 'reptiles' as we now know the term? Or were they as efficient in their physiology as mammals? Could they run fast, and for long periods? Were they, in fact, 'hot-blooded' as opposed to 'cold-blooded'? If so, when did this fortunate trait evolve?

Another issue is: if they were so successful, why should they have died out, leaving the earth to the apparently insignificant mammals that had inhabited the earth for the previous 200 million years—minute shrew-like creatures scampering, climbing or burrowing to safety at the approach of huge reptilian feet?

A third issue arose when many scientists noted that those that walked on their back legs had feet very like those of birds, many had hips like birds and some were similar to early birds in their skeletal structure. Could it be that birds are in fact nothing but tiny versions of feathered dinosaurs?

The answers to these questions are by no means certain. But it is likely that the search for certainty will involve a drastic re-think of the way many groups of animals—both extinct and modern—are understood and classified.

1 The Coming of the Dinosaurs

Where did the dinosaurs come from? How did they live? How were they all related? Why did they vanish from the earth? These are the questions that scientists have asked for over a century, and are still asking. We do now have some answers in general terms, but to understand them we have to set the dinosaurs in the context of the history of the earth.

The earth was formed about 4500 million years ago. The first rocks of which we have records are 3750 million years old. When they were formed there was no life—just the brownish rock, glinting with spots of mineral, torn by volcanoes, rent by earthquakes and scoured by the teeming rains that formed the ancient seas. Only the earth, the sea and the air moved. Nothing on land could have survived the sun's ultraviolet radiation, which poured through the ammonia and methane of the primitive atmosphere.

Looming up in a glade at London's Crystal Palace, this 1854 reconstruction—the first—is a replica of Iguanodon, *showing it as a quadruped, not a biped.*

The surface of the earth, however, possessed the basic ingredients of life—carbon, hydrogen, oxygen and nitrogen. Perhaps fired by bolts of lightning, these chemicals were recast to form more complex molecules that in turn recombined to make the first molecules that could reproduce themselves. These microscopic organisms sustained themselves by fermentation in the chemicals of the ocean, giving off carbon dioxide. They became the basis for new forms of life, containing chlorophyll, the ingredient in the process of photosynthesis that permits the manufacture of sugar from carbon dioxide, water and sunlight.

Thus freed from dependence upon waterborne chemicals, the first plants arose. A by-product of photosynthesis is oxygen, which plants cannot use. For hundreds of millions of years, oxygen seeped into the atmosphere, slowly transforming it. A thousand million years ago—when the earth's history to the present had already run three-quarters of its course—there arose microscopic animals that could make use of the oxygen. Over millions of years, these evolved into ancient sponges, jellyfish, worms, corals and shellfish.

The shellfish left the first true fossils. They arose during the Cambrian period, which lasted some 100 million years. The Cambrian is the first period in the second of four great eras into which the history of the earth is divided. These four are the Pre-Cambrian (without life), the Paleozoic (with ancient forms of life), the Mesozoic (the age of the dinosaurs) and the Cenozoic (to the present). The Paleozoic lasted about 400 million years and during that time there arose the first creatures with external skeltons, the first fish and the first amphibians.

Plants evolved that could make increasingly good use of the power of the sun and thus could grow on land. Gradually the first horsetails, leafless shrubs and ferns gave rise to more efficient seed-bearing plants such as the early spruces, firs and pines. As the forests spread they were colonized by the first insects, similar to dragonflies and cockroaches. Amphibians, which had to moisten their skins regularly and lay their eggs in water, gave way to reptiles, which were independent of the water, and laid their eggs on land. In the Permian Period, which closed the Paleozoic Era 225 million years ago, the reptiles were the dominant large terrestrial creatures.

Reptiles have a number of advantages over their amphibian predecessors which opened up a new range of possible habitats. For example, amphibians have naked skins without hair, scales or other protective devices, so they are

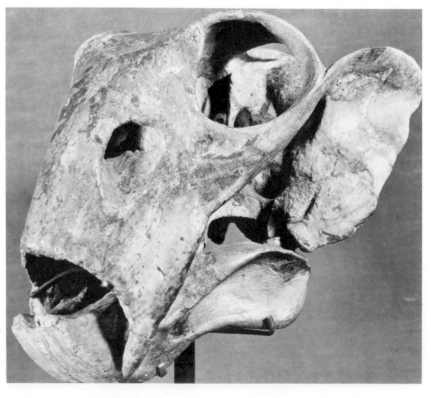

Lystrosaurus was a four-foot reptile, solidly built, as this skull suggests, which roamed widely in the southern hemisphere in early Triassic times.

Two sunburned paleontologists dig up Coelophysis *bones in New Mexico.*

apt to dry out and must remain near water for survival. Reptiles have a horny skin with scales that lessens the chance of drying. Also, amphibians lay eggs that are soft and gelatin-like, making them prone to drying out. But the reptilian egg is built more solidly—with a shell—and thus can be laid anywhere *except* in water.

Reptiles began to spread rapidly. From the early carnivores that preyed on each other and more primitive creatures, the first herbivorous reptiles developed. Carnivores face a problem —there is a limited amount of other animals to eat. Herbivores have an almost unlimited supply of plants to eat.

Three main branches on the evolutionary tree developed from the early reptiles—modern reptiles, the mammal-like reptiles and the dinosaurs. The dinosaur line arose during the late Permian, some 225 million years ago, and in the beginning formed a group known as the Archosaurs, or 'ruling reptiles'. They evolved for the next 30 million years into a group called the Thecodonts. The Thecodonts gave rise to four major groups: crocodiles, birds, flying reptiles and dinosaurs.

The Thecodonts were completely new types of creatures, as their name—which means 'socket tooth'—implies. Their teeth were not, as is the case with lizards, fused to the jaw but were individually rooted and could be replaced. These animals also had the ability to lose heat.

They almost certainly had no insulation—fat, fur or feathers.

The Thecodonts had greater speed than their predecessors. Some of them began to run on two legs only. Their size ranged from goose-sized lightweights to 80-ton giants. Some of them were able to fly. Some of them stayed in the water all their lives.

The best known of the early Thecodonts was a crocodile-like creature called *Proterosuchus*. It was only about five feet long but it had a powerful battery of teeth and spent its life swimming in the shallows hunting for fish, or waddling on the shore where it probably fed on another type of Thecodont, *Lystrosaurus*. The descendants of *Proterosuchus* evolved into solid, scaly creatures, some of which could easily have been mistaken for crocodiles.

The first Thecodont that was able to raise itself off the ground and develop limbs that were tucked under the body for more efficiency and more speed may have been a *Cheirotherium*. The name means 'hand-mammal'. This animal is known only from its footprints, which look something like those of a mammal, with four solid fingers and a 'thumb' that sticks out to the side. It must have been about nine feet in length, held itself clear of the ground and its limbs must have been held directly underneath its body.

Euparkeria was a small creature, only two or three feet long, but it was remarkable in that

ABOVE: *The fossil footprints of a* Cheirotherium *look like the imprints of a human hand. It may have been a dinosaur.* BELOW: *In the background is* Ornithosuchus *(ten feet long) and in the foreground is* Euparkeria *(three feet long).*

its front legs were much shorter than its back legs and it possibly ran on its hind feet. *Ornithosuchus*, another Triassic animal, was up to 12 feet long and also ran on its hind feet when chasing small reptiles for its food. It probably grabbed them with its fore-feet. This reptile, whose name means 'the bird crocodile', was the ancestor of all the large flesh-eating dinosaurs.

Coelophysis was from eight to ten feet in length and probably weighed only 40 or 50 pounds. Its bones were hollow and contained air sacs like the bones of birds. It had a long

neck and delicate, saw-tooth teeth. It also ran on its hind feet.

The Thecodonts 'invented' the upright pose—one of the most momentous changes in biological design in the history of the world. They and their successors could now choose between fast movement over the ground—on the basis of vertical limbs that supported them without much use of muscular energy—or could opt for greater size and ultimately a return to the four-footed stance—an option that eventually led to the huge multi-ton monsters of children's picture books.

In the background is Ornithosuchus,, *which is often considered to be the first true dinosaur. It was bipedal. In the foreground is* Coelophysis, *a nimble animal with a long tail and a small head. It, too, was a biped and preyed on smaller creatures.*

2 The First Ruling Reptiles

By the late Triassic, 200 million years ago, the early dinosaurs had almost completely taken over the land from the Thecodonts. They began to evolve into larger species, and that size offered protection against predators and allowed them to preserve a stable temperature. There emerged a range of dinosaurs that can be divided into four types: large and small herbivores and large and small carnivores.

The best known of the early plant-eaters is *Plateosaurus*. Measuring up to 20 feet in length, *Plateosaurus* was one of the first dinosaurs to show some bulk. Its broadly arched ribs and its bulging abdomen gave it a barrel-like appearance. It had stout hind limbs and broad hind feet with four strong forward-pointing toes. Its fore-limbs were also strong enough to help it in walking and standing, but when running and feeding, it must have reared itself up on its hind-limbs. Its teeth were blunt—ideal for eating small vegetation—and its long neck and small head were typical of the even bigger plant-eaters that were its probable descendants. But it also had clawed fingers and hands that were turned inward—suitable for catching and holding small prey. What it ate is still being argued.

Powerful predatory meat-eaters were also common in the late Triassic. A typical one was *Teratosaurus*. Although nowhere nearly as fearsome as the later giant carnivores, it was still a sizable 20 feet long and must have weighed a half ton. Its neck was fairly short, its back legs bulky and it had a long tail to counter-balance its heavy body. It had three-toed feet with heavy hook-like claws—perhaps an adaptation for grasping or slashing prey. *Teratosaurus* had a large heavy skull furnished with vicious blade-like teeth.

During the Jurassic the smallest dinosaur known appeared—*Compsognathus*. This little animal was hardly more than two feet in length and had a skeleton extraordinarily similar to that of the first bird, *Archaeopteryx*.

RIGHT: *Skeletons of* Iguanodons *in Brussels'*
Royal Museum. They were discovered by
coal miners in 1878 near Bernissart, Belgium
and were reconstructed by Louis Dollo.
LEFT: *Dollo's workmen reconstructing an*
Iguanodon *in 1880 in a chapel being used*
temporarily as a museum workshop. Today
there are 11 complete standing skeletons in
the museum along with a score of partial ones.

RIGHT: Plateosaurus, *20 feet long, has solid forelimbs that suggest that it was partly quadrupedal, but they were also short, which suggests that it could rear up on two legs to eat.*
ABOVE: A skeleton of a Plateosaurus.

A larger dinosaur at that time was *Ornitholestes,* or 'bird-robber'. These slender seven-foot creatures had long, slim, strong clawed fingers, suitable for capturing active and elusive prey such as birds or small lizards and mammals.

The Jurassic also saw the evolution of the first of the giant flesh-eaters, such as *Megalosaurus,* which was the first dinosaur ever named. They were solid creatures, varying from 10 to 25 feet in length. The head was about a foot long and the teeth were shaped like miniature steak knives—laid back into the mouth like shark's teeth—anything gripped in the jaws would have little chance to escape. The short, stout neck and the powerful back legs must have enabled it, like a shark, to grab great chunks of flesh in its mouth and tear them off with shakes of the head and body.

There was also the *Allosaurus,* which grew over 40 feet long and had three-toed feet. The feet were shaped like those of a bird but ended in formidable clawed talons with which the animal could have torn apart its prey to get at the entrails in a matter of seconds. It weighed two tons and its footprints show that it had a six-foot stride.

The large flesh-eaters, by and large, had to combine lightness of skull with strength. Muscles were needed to tear their prey and the less weight they had to carry in their skulls the better. Therefore, like many other dinosaurs, they had quite thin skulls, and despite the size of the skull, the brain was no larger than that of a kitten. The bones at the back of the skull were loosely jointed, snake-like, to allow for a wide range of movement when the animal swallowed large chunks of flesh. In addition, the long powerful tail was used both as a balance and as a weapon to lash out at rivals for a kill.

The dinosaurs that everyone knows were the great plant-eaters such as *Diplodocus*, *Apatosaurus* (which used to be called *Bronto-*

saurus) and the largest of all, *Brachiosaurus*. There were many types of these huge creatures, but they all had the same ground plan—massive bodies, long necks, long tails, tiny heads and pillar-like legs. They weighed from one to 80 tons.

Diplodocus is perhaps the best known of all the dinosaurs. It was a light creature in comparison to its length. It weighed not much more than 10 tons, for it was mostly neck (22 feet) and tail (50 1/2 feet). The tail petered out

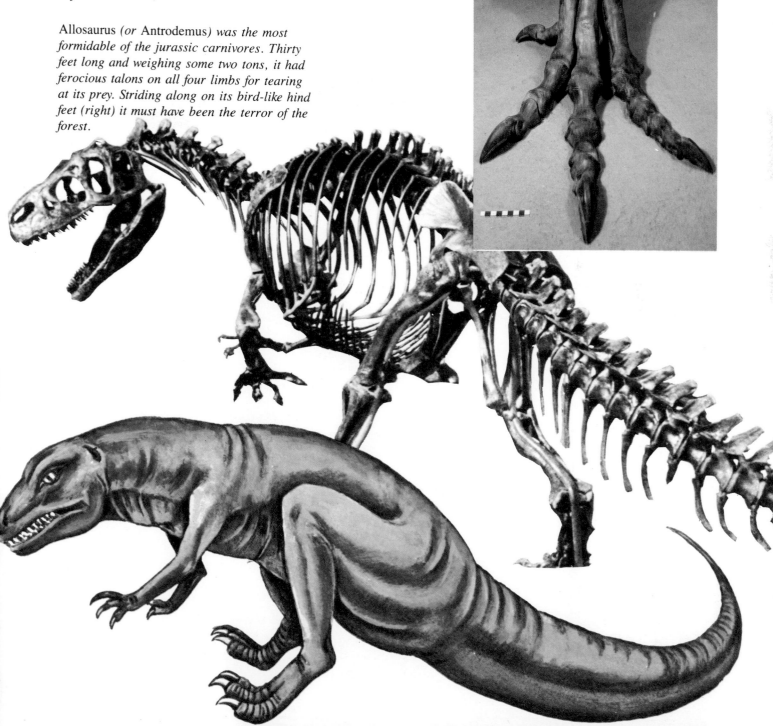

Allosaurus (*or* Antrodemus) *was the most formidable of the jurassic carnivores. Thirty feet long and weighing some two tons, it had ferocious talons on all four limbs for tearing at its prey. Striding along on its bird-like hind feet (right) it must have been the terror of the forest.*

into tiny vertebrae, no wider than bones of a human little finger. The neck, like the head of a crane, was kept suspended in the air without any muscular effort by great cables of tendons attached to the shoulders. The tendons ran from powerful muscles up the neck vertebrae into the top of the head.

Diplodocus and others of its kind were marvelous creations, from an engineering point of view. The problems of being a giant are considerable. Whales survive happily enough in the water because they are supported by their own environment. If stranded on a beach, however, they rapidly suffocate under their own weight—a whale's skeleton is not strong enough to support it and its lungs are crushed. *Diplodocus* was built like a bridge. The back was arched and the legs were pillar-like supports that plunged straight down. The problem of excess bulk was solved.

The great plant-eaters, except for *Brachiosaurus,* all had front legs that were shorter than the hind legs. Their legs were very like those of elephants, with short, heavy toe-bones and an extended pad behind and beneath the bones of the foot to take up the shock of impact. Calculations have shown that the legs of the *Diplodocus* have a safety factor of four—that is, it could have supported its whole weight on one leg, or even borne the weight of three other *Diplodoci* on its back. An 80-ton *Brachiosaurus,* mathematically, would therefore be able to support a burden of a couple of hundred tons if it were correctly loaded.

It used to be commonly assumed that these huge creatures spent most of their life in water to avoid the necessity of having to support their giant weight on land. If elephants are the largest land animals known today, it was thought, how could the giant dinosaurs have grown so much larger unless they were supported by water? Besides, the nasal openings of most of them were high up on the head so that they could breathe by sticking just their

heads above water. They would also have been able to escape the carnivorous animals that patrolled the shorelines. Finally, these dinosaurs typically had weak, rake-like teeth that could have been used for hauling up masses of soft, dense, tropical water vegetation.

But remember that the bones of these creatures were built for lightness. The skeleton of a giant herbivorous dinosaur typically weighs about half that of a whale skeleton of the same size. Lightness of skeleton is a walking, or running, or flying adaptation and not at all a swimming one.

Breathing while their bodies were immersed in deep water could also have been a problem to these beasts. Humans cannot breathe through a tube in water that is more than three or four feet deep. At that depth, the water pressure on the lungs becomes too great and the chest muscles simply cannot operate. Even whales cannot breathe in unless they are lying flat on the surface of the water. It was calcu-

lated, therefore, that a *Diplodocus* standing at a depth of 30 feet would be subjected to pressure on its body of about double that of ordinary atmospheric pressure. To overcome such pressure, the muscles of the repiratory system would have needed to generate tremendous power—so much that these muscles would have weighed several tons. There are no bones that would have acted as a framework for such muscles.

A skeleton of the giant plant-eater Diplodocus *—at almost 90 feet the longest land creature ever—weighed a mere 10 tons. Its neck and back vertebrae were hollow.*

It was finally concluded that these creatures were not water animals by nature. They were more likely to have been plains-dwellers, rarely venturing into the water.

The Jurassic also saw the development of the first 'bird-hipped' dinosaurs—those that were to evolve in later ages into the upright herbivores such as *Iguanodon* and a wide variety of armored dinosaurs. This type had first emerged during Triassic times with the *Fabrosaurus*. The line had not proved particularly dramatic but it had endured and now emerged in one of the most intriguing of the smaller dinosaurs, *Hypsilophodon*. This nimble creature, four or five feet long, was a fast mover. In some ways it was primitive, in that it retained a five-fingered hand and a foot with four very long toes. Like other bird-hipped species, it possessed the tendons that kept the tail rigid to be used as a stabilizer sticking out behind.

Hypsilophodon, because it seemed to have such good fingers and toes, was first thought to have been a tree-climbing reptile that ate fruit and leaves. But it was recently discovered that

BELOW: This 12-inch fossil jawbone, on display in the Oxford Museum in England, is part of the first dinosaur to be scientifically described, in 1824. It was a Megalosaurus.

BOTTOM: A nineteenth century painting of a Megalosaurus bucklandi *guarding its newly-killed prey from two of its relatives. It is wrongly depicted as a quadruped and the artist obviously used a lion as his model.*

For such a mountain of flesh and bone, the head of the Brachiosaurus *might seem to be strangely small.*

its back feet could not have gripped branches, although it nevertheless might have climbed into trees as a defense against predators, or to feed as goats do. (Goats are extremely good climbers.) However it lived, it was certainly extremely effective and remained unchanged almost until the extinction of the dinosaurs themselves.

The first of the large, upright, bird-hipped plant-eater was *Camptosaurus*—a 15-foot, three-ton creature. It was like a primitive *Iguanodon;* it had curved thigh bones—as opposed to the *Iguanodon's* straight ones—

The Brachiosaurus *had massive limbs that equipped it for life on land.*

and probably therefore tended to lower itself on four legs a good deal. It had a long, flat head with ridged and closely-packed teeth that were adapted for crushing plants. It also had a bony beak-like ridge instead of a lower lip.

The floor of its lower jaw was grooved, perhaps to contain a long tongue that could whip out, seize plants, then retract to allow the plants to be sliced off by the hard beak before the food was chopped up by the teeth. It also had elastic cheeks—an adaptation possessed now only by mammals—which allowed it to take much larger mouthfuls and chew its food over and over again before swallowing it. This made for efficient digestion.

During the Jurassic there also evolved the first of the heavily protected dinosaurs. Various defenses had already been evolved—size, aggressiveness, herding, fleetness of foot—and there now emerged a new range of adaptations which evolved as 'hands off' protection against the giant carnivores. The way was shown by *Scelidosaurus*, a four-legged relative of *Fabrosaurus*. *Scelidosaurus* had two claims to fame. Along its 12-foot body it had small triangular spikes, a hint of the heavy armor that was to enclose its descendants. It also lacked in its bird-hip the forward prong that defined the hips of its descendants.

The teeth of *Scelidosaurus*—close-set, cylindrical, with a flowershaped crown—offer a clue to its way of life. Its remains were found in marine sediments, and it was first thought that the animal would have been equally happy munching up sea-side vegetation or swimming out to look for marine prey. Now, however, it seems more likely that it was purely vegetarian and that it lived on soft plants by the edges of rivers and lagoons.

Two of the oddest-looking lines of dinosaurs emerged after *Scelidosaurus*. They were the spikiest, *Kentrosaurus,* and perhaps the strangest of all, *Stegosaurus.*

Kentrosaurus was a quadruped with an extraordinary protective line of spikes down its backbone. The spikes ran in pairs, with an extra pair sticking out of its hips. Those that ran down its tail must have made formidable weapons.

In *Stegosaurus*, the spikes had evolved into huge plates, making the creature into one of the most recognizable of all the dinosaurs. *Stegosaurus*, a bulky plant-eater weighing nearly two tons, is still something of a puzzle. The creature had ridiculously short front legs and yet it always walked on all fours. The thigh bones in its hind leg were remarkably long, about the size of an elephant's thigh bone and about twice the size of its lower leg bones which made it look as if its knees were much too low for comfort. It also had a tiny skull.

Its most remarkable features were the great plates that flowed down its back—triangular bony outgrowths that turned into spikes toward the rear, of which the tail had two pairs. It was first thought that the plates stuck up in the air in pairs, and this idea was quite controversial. No plates had been found in pairs in fossil remains, and no one could think of a good purpose for the plates. If they were supposed to be a defense, it would have been easy enough for a predator to move up alongside the creature and tear away at its flanks.

Besides, they were set into the skin, not the skeleton, and could not have been all that rigid. Later a skeleton was found with the plates fossilized not in pairs but alternatively. Perhaps the alternation of the plates reflected the conditions of fossilization, not the creature's actual appearance.

Many scientists now tend to think that the plates were set flat, flopping over sideways to cover the flanks. Even so they could hardly have been very effective for their size. Perhaps they helped radiate heat; but why should the Stegosaurs, of which there were many different species, need radiators when other large dinosaurs did not? Or perhaps they were some bizarre sexual characteristic, a dinosaurian version of the weird and colorful plumes that define the many species of the birds of paradise in present-day New Guinea.

The beast was an oddity in other ways as well. Its head was not much bigger than that of an Alsatian dog and its brain was the size of a walnut. Whatever the qualities of many of the dinosaurs, it is difficult to think of the Stegosaur as a particularly bright creature.

When Stegosaur fossils were first discovered, it was noticed that there were enlargements to the spinal cord in the pelvic region. Such enlargements were a common feature of many dinosaurs, but in *Stegosaurus* that cavity was 20 times the size of the brain proper. It was at first assumed that the dinosaur needed the enlargement as a local nerve center—or second brain—to control the movements of the great back legs.

In fact, the enlargement of the area through which the spinal column ran was probably a gland which may have stored glycogen, or animal starch, a chemical used in muscular reactions, and could thus have been a store of ready energy for emergencies. The ostrich has a similar glycogen gland in the same part of its body—a possible reminder of its far distant relationship to the dinosaurs.

The Stegosaurs were a wide-spread group of dinosaurs. Remains of them have been found in Africa, Europe and North America. But they became extinct shortly after the end of the Jurassic; why, no one knows. It may have had something to do with the changes that marked the beginning of the Cretaceous. The seas began to rise and eventually divided the continents into two continental islands. If the Stegosaur's plates really were an adaptation to heat, it is possible that the increasing humidity that must have accompanied the end of the first great age of dinosaurs simply changed the environment to which the animal had adapted, making it impossible for *Stegosaurus* to survive.

LEFT: Kentrosaurus *was an East African stegosaur. Its spikes were less formidable than they look because they were not part of the skeleton but were attached to the skin.*
BELOW: Scientists are still not certain how the plates of Stegosaurus—*one of the most popular of all the dinosaurs—would have looked in real life. They are usually restored sticking up in a great frill, but in this position they would have offered little defense.*

3 The Golden Age

The Cretaceous, from about 136 to 65 million years ago, was a period of great change in some areas. But in the south there was little change. The great Jurassic herbivores and carnivores lived on—if in reduced numbers—to the end of the Cretaceous. In the north more intense evolutionary pressures favored the bird-hipped type of dinosaur. The great herbivores and carnivores went into a decline and new and weird types of herbivores evolved—tank-like Ankylosaurs with clubbed tails, dinosaurs with horns and frills, duck-billed dinosaurs.

Environmental changes—most significantly, perhaps, the spread of the flowering plants which were established by the mid-Cretaceous—provided more varied environments for the dinosaurs. But such diversity proved to be of no avail. Not a single dinosaur survived beyond the end of the Cretaceous.

The natural world in the Cretaceous would have seemed much more familiar to us than the

Lifelike models of a mother and baby Triceratops—*one of the most successful of later dinosaur species—shown standing by a waterhole in the Hamburg Zoo in West Germany.*

Jurassic. Gingko trees and conifers, already ancient species, were common. But newly evolved pines, firs, oaks, ash, poplars, sycamores and willows also dotted the landscape. In the undergrowth, magnolia bushes and viburnum thrived; holly had appeared for the first time; there were climbing plants such as roses, grape vines and passion flowers; banks of saxifrage provided patches of cover, along with euphorbias and heather. Many of the landscapes would have been splashed with the colors and scents that we know today.

The new kinds of plants provided new living places for small creatures. Bees and other insects evolved their peculiar relationship with the flowers, feeding on them and pollinating them. And—perhaps the most telling change of all for a time traveler—there were birds: the gull-like (but toothed) *Hesperornis*, the speedy tern-like *Ichthyornis* and species that resembled cormorants, divers, herons, rails and moorhens.

Other groups of animals, too, evolved into forms we know today. Snakes appeared (although, apparently, not poisonous ones). The lizards diversified. The mammals slowly developed from the shrew-like creatures of the early Jurassic to varied (yet still small) creatures that resembled possums and hedgehogs. There even appeared, late in the Cretaceous, a tree-shrew, an aggressive solitary little creature that has survived to the present time. This was the most remote ancestor of the primates, the line that includes the monkeys and apes and, of course, man himself.

Scientists now have a good idea of the evolution of the dinosaurs during the Cretaceous. The great plant-eaters continued much as they had always done, evolving new species that were in many respects the same as the old ones. These giant plant-eaters were fed upon by two-footed, lizard-hipped predators which now evolved into the most ferocious carnivorous animals of all time. The biggest of all, and the one known to almost every child above the age of three, was *Tyrannosaurus rex*—'the king of the tyrant reptiles.' This creature, by the way, is the only dinosaur that is popularly know by its full scientific name, rather than by its single generic name.

T rex was certainly a most amazing creature. It measured over 40 feet from snout to tail and it carried its head some 17 feet above the ground. This is a considerable height—three times that of a human being and almost on a level with the world pole vault record. It is possible that really large Tyrannosaurs weighed 10 tons.

The Tyrannosaur had a four-foot skull and teeth that could reach six inches long and an inch wide. The teeth were serrated along their edges and curved inwards. Each of the teeth, of which there were several dozen, was like a small curved dagger, sharp and serrated like steak knives on both sides. Its powerful back legs raised the beast's hip region 10 feet off the ground; its knee would have been level with a human head. No wonder it has been the star of so many monster movies, striding across the land, spreading fear and destruction in its wake.

In fact its traditional image has been slightly modified. It used to be portrayed towering in an upright pose, with a long tail which swung about or trailed on the ground. Actually its tail was relatively short and bulky and since it must have helped in the animal's balance, it

When Tyrannosaurus rex *was restored (right), its forearms—tiny, but well-muscled and with two pointed claws—posed a problem. They could not have been used in killing or eating. One theory suggests that they were used to establish balance when the animal stood up (below). The claws may have acted as a brake to prevent the creature from sliding forward as it reared to an upright position.*

was probably held above the ground. Like others of its kind, the Tyrannosaur probably did not walk upright, but horizontally, its tail acting as a counterbalance to its body.

With that great bulk to carry, it did not even run. Footprints of Tyrannosaurs have been found and they show that it had a stride only about three feet long. It also has been suggested that it would not have been an active predator—it would not have pursued and killed its prey. First, it could not move fast enough; almost all dinosaurs would have been able to outrun it. Secondly, even if it had caught and attacked a victim, its teeth were for eating, not for killing. They would have snapped off in the battle and would not have been available to perform their first function of providing meat for the animal.

The vicious claws that capped its toes would certainly have been capable of tearing open even the largest of the giant plant-eaters, but to tackle a live and active one would have demanded a one-legged kick, a feat of balancing skill outside *Tyrannosaurus rex's* repertoire. The claws may have been used to dismember corpses but were probably most useful in retaining a good foothold. Those who cannot bear to see the king dethroned should be reassured: the view that Tyrannosaurus was a carrion eater and not a killer is by no means

LEFT: A life-sized tyrannosaur tooth reveals minute steak-knife serrations along the cutting edge. BELOW: These comparative models show Tyrannosaurus rex's *bulk. A human would scarcely reached its knee cap.*

universally held. Many paleontologists still see the creature as a predator.

The really odd thing about the Tyrannosaur is the size of its forearms. They were only a couple of feet long, smaller than human arms. They certainly could not have been used to sieze prey or to help in the tearing up of food. In addition they seem to have been highly specialized: they had only two fingers, as opposed to the usual three, and they were long and spindly. It was once suggested that they were used as toothpicks but the dinosaur could not even reach its mouth with them. No one has yet found a real use for the delicate front claws. But it is possible that the fore-limbs were used to shift the weight backwards, over the back legs, as the beast got up from the prone position.

The evidence for this theory lies in the fact that the tiny limb with its well-developed claws was supported by a strong pectoral girdle, indicating that it was well supplied with muscles. It might have rested by squatting down, chicken fashion, its legs tucked underneath its body. If from this position it simply straightened its legs to get up, it might have overbalanced forward, or simply pushed its head along the ground, without ever getting upright. Conceivably the claws of the front legs locked into the ground, giving it a slight but necessary backwards purchase, allowing the animal to throw its head back and then straighten its legs.

The later carnivores were not all huge, however, some were small and almost certainly active predators. One, *Deinontychus*, is of particular importance. It was a lightly built dinosaur that stood on its hind legs, nine feet long from head to tail. The tail was long and was locked out behind the body by a series of ossified rods. It probably carried its head four feet above the ground. *Deinontychus* means 'terrible claw'—an apt name, for it walked only on two of its three claws. The third was held several inches off the ground and was modified into a lethal five-inch sickleshaped talon.

To use it, the dinosaur must have been extremely agile; in addition to being a fast runner, it must have been able to stand on one leg and use its other leg, karate fashion, to slash at its would-be prey. Its arms, too, were long and equipped with claws, so that it could either grapple its prey to its chest or hold it at arms' length to disembowel it with a kick.

It is possible that *Deinonychus* is a representative of a whole group of dinosaurs yet to be discovered. In 1965 a pair of huge forearms were found in Mongolia, very much like those

The extraordinary domed skulls and the bony nodules of the pachycephalosaurs, or 'thick-headed' dinosaurs, have long puzzled scientists. The skulls, several inches thick, may have evolved for ritual head-to-head charges.

of *Deinonychus,* except four times the size. The animal was named *Deinocheirus* ('terrible hand') and if it really was a larger version of *Deinonychus* it would have been even more formidable than *Tyrannosaurus rex.* Imagine a 12-foot-high creature able to run at 30 to 40 mph, with sickle claws two feet long on its feet! But in fact such a creature would not probably have been able to move with corresponding speed and it is possible that the huge forearms belonged to a different sort of animal altogether —as yet unidentified.

Just as the giant carnivores increased in size, so did the light, swift-moving meat-eaters. The small bird-like dinosaurs of earlier times developed into large 'ostrich dinosaurs,' the best known of which are *Ornithomimus* and *Struthiomimus.* Both were indeed very like ostriches. They had long legs, compact bodies, long necks, hooked beaks and could undoubtedly run very fast. Of course they had fore-legs instead of wings, a reptilian tail and no feathers but they probably ate both flesh and plants, as ostriches do today, and could survive either by snatching up young dinosaurs or picking fruit off trees with their long, agile fore-limbs.

The most dramatic development in the Cretaceous was the extension in range of the bird-hipped dinosaurs, all herbivores. One successful type was the *Iguanodon* and its relatives in North America and Africa. One *Iguanodon* relative was found to have a sail-like fin down its back. It was found near the equator in Africa and a fin extensively supplied with blood vessels may have helped it to radiate excess heat and thus preserve its efficiency.

A second group of bird-hipped dinosaurs was the armored creatures of which *Stegosaurus* was the ancestor. Although Stegosaurs became extinct in the early Cretaceous, their relatives, the Ankylosaurs, proved extremely efficient. *Ankylosaurus* itself, the animal that the group was named after, was armored with flat plates which were fused to its skin all over the top of its body. Weighing some three tons, *Ankylosaurus* must have scurried along under its tank-like armor plating almost immune from assault. It had stocky legs and a bony lump on the end of its tail which could have dealt a very nasty blow.

Other creatures in the same group developed variations on this theme, protecting themselves with spikes, plates and other outgrowths. Ankylosaurs roamed all over North America, Europe and Asia and survived successfully right up to the end of the Cretaceous.

A third group of bird-hipped dinosaurs was dome-headed. These, the Pachycephalosaurs, the 'thick-headed reptiles', had skulls several inches thick but were quite delicately built otherwise, with no natural defenses. They may have filled the niches occupied nowadays by sheep, goats or ibexes. They are little represented in the fossil records and therefore, since fossils tend to occur most frequently in lowlands where sediments are laid down, the dome-heads possibly inhabited uplands away from the larger predators.

That possibility at least suggests a reason for their thickened heads which were well-rounded and would have been of little use in attack or defense. The skulls could have been the dinosaurian equivalent of a ram's horns today. Males may have squared off to engage in ritual battle at mating time. Perhaps the mountainous regions of Asia and North America echoed in springtime to the clash of bone meeting bone as a dome-headed male charged and butted another dome-headed male into submission for the possession of a herd of docile females.

Yet another group of bird-hipped dinosaurs were the Hadrosaurs or duck-billed dinosaurs, named for their rounded upper jaw which was flattened at the tip. The front edge of the bills were curved over in a sort of beak. Clearly the Hadrosaurs could have consumed a wide variety of plant life and were well suited to dealing with the tough flowering plants that had evolved by the late Cretaceous.

The stomach contents of a mummified 'duck-reptile', *Anatosaurus,* were found in 1922. Not long before its death, the creature had eaten a meal of conifer needles, twigs, fruit and seeds. To cope with their diet, the Hadrosaurs' jaws were most unusual. They had batteries of teeth, so the upper and lower jaws ground together like millstones. *Anatosaurus* had up to 60 rows of teeth on each jaw, each containing six or more layers, one above the other, which would be used in succession as the outside layer wore away. An *Anatosaurus* had over 1200 teeth in its head. The food was continuously pressed back between the jaws by elastic cheek pouches.

Many of the Hadrosaurs had webbed hands and flattened tails, indicating that they spent some of their lives in water. Many species were flat-headed, many others had crests, of which some were solid-crested. Some of the solid crested Hadrosaurs developed spikes that ran back from the brows and struck out of the crown of the head. In others, the spike ran forwards. In the hollow crested species, many had dramatic crests that swept back like the plumes in a cavalier's hat. The space inside the crest was connected with the nasal passages.

Edmontosaurus, *a hadrosaur with a flat head and duck bill typical of this widespread and successful family. Here it stands in the muddy shallows eating tough rush plants.*

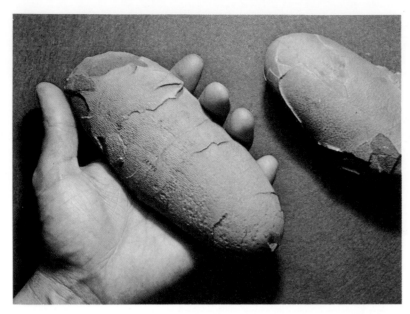

LEFT: *The eggs of an early frilled dinosaur,* Proceratops, *which were found in the Gobi Desert. The eggs were laid in large pits in concentric circles.* BELOW: *Possibly the female then covered the eggs with sand, as turtles do, and allowed the young to hatch out in the heat of the sun—a scene shown in the model.*

The nasal passages were probably connected with the Hadrosaurs' sense of smell. In the late Cretaceous landscape, which contained so many new varieties of plants, any device that would help a species find a new home by allowing it to concentrate on a new food source would offer a new evolutionary advantage. Different species could then have co-existed without direct competition for food. The crests of the Hadrosaurs and the air passages they contained could have vastly extended the skin surface available for analyzing smells. Since the Hadrosaurs lacked defensive weapons, a delicate sense of smell would have allowed them to scent a potential predator in good time to flee.

If so, they must have depended on their other senses as well. Perhaps they had color vision to distinguish their food sources, their own kind and possible predators. Almost certainly they had a good sense of hearing. One Hadrosaur skull has been found with the bone of the middle ear preserved. This bone, only 2.5 millimeters wide at its thickest, was so delicate that it must have been sensitive to very small vibrations.

We get a picture of Hadrosaurs as living rather as hoofed mammals do today in Southern Africa—a huge variety of species co-existing in interlinking communities, some feeding on grasses, some on bushes, some on trees. They are vulnerable to predators but alert to the slightest danger and skittishly ready to heave themselves out of harm's way.

The final group of bird-hipped dinosaurs is the Ceratopsians 'horned-eye' or 'horned-face.' The first Ceratopsian ever discovered was *Protoceratops,* a dinosaur that traveled on four legs. It was seven feet in length and carried a very solid skull that was almost as long as its back. It had a heavy frill, or shield, that extended back from the skull over the neck and shoulders. This frill, which characterized all the horned dinosaurs, had a number of functions. It acted as an attachment for the jaw and neck muscles and provided protection for the neck and back. The skull itself had a parrot-like look to it because the top jaw was hooked. But it also had a small bump on the midline of the nose—a foreshadowing of the horns that were to decorate its descendants.

Its eggs were about eight inches in length —larger relatively than any reptile's eggs today —and oblong, like the eggs of modern lizards. The shells had a speckled look and probably were leathery when laid. They were found in clutches which indicated that they had been set

Prosaurolophus *teeth were beveled and were constantly being replaced throughout the animal's life. The whole set of several hundred teeth could serve as cutters and grinders.*

out in nests. Clearly *Protoceratops* females were comparable in their behavior to modern turtles—they dug hollows in the sand, deposited a dozen or so eggs in a circle and then covered the eggs with sand until they hatched.

Dinosaur eggs suggest some intriguing thoughts about how those animals lived. The largest egg yet found belonged to a medium-sized, 35-foot Cretaceous plant-eater, *Hypselosaurus*. The 12-inch long egg could have contained about five and one-half pints— twice the size of an ostrich egg but half the size of the largest known egg, that of the extinct Madagascan elephant bird, which was 28 inches around, about the limit in size for an egg. Beyond this point any shell, which must remain permeable to the gases that help nourish the embryo, collapses under gravitational pressure.

The odd thing about these eggs is the enormous disparity between the size of the hatchlings and the adult. An ostrich egg is about 1/60th the weight of the adult. An adult crocodile weighs 2000 times as much as its egg. *Hypselosaurus* would have to multiply its weight some 5000 to 10,000 times in growing up. If this were possible, what of the giant plant-eating dinosaurs? If they moved about in herds, what happened to the youngsters? Did they rear themselves from birth? Or did some of these dinosaurs simply drop live young, as many hoofed mammals do now, which would have joined the herd?

After *Protoceratops* the horned dinosaurs grew in size and developed their frills until there were two distinct families defined by long and short frills. Ten million years after *Protoceratops* lived, a single-horned rhinoceros-type creature called *Monoclonius,* some 16 to 18 feet long, colonized North America. Some 10 or 15 million years later still, the same area was home to *Triceratops* ('three-horned eye'), a massive 24-foot long herbivore that weighed over eight tons.

It had an enormous horn over each eye and a shorter one on its nose, and its bony neck frill reached well back over its shoulders. *Triceratops* must have filled a role comparable to a combination of buffalo and elephant, and wandered in herds of many thousands across

the late Cretaceous landscape of North America, probably surrounding the young to present a formidable battery of spikes for any would-be predators such *Tyrannosaurus rex*. Armed with long horns on a highly maneuverable head, strong beaks, and the ability to

gallop at speeds probably up to 30 mph, these large Ceratopsians must have been some of the most dangerous terrestrial herbivores ever to have evolved. They survived right until the end of the dinosaurian times and then vanished rapidly.

Triceratops, *30 feet long and weighing eight tons, was the largest of its family and one of the last dinosaurs. The bony frill was, in early species, an attachment for powerful jaw muscles, but in later species it is thought that it probably also served as a shield.*

4 Rulers of Sea & Air

The success of the great reptiles was not limited to the land. Early in their evolution they recolonized the seas and took to the air. The sea-dwellers were not all that closely related to the dinosaurs—they evolved long before even the earliest dinosaurs had emerged—but they are very much a part of the dinosaur story, for the large marine reptiles died out at the same time as the dinosaurs themselves and any account of their extinction must take the disappearance of the marine reptiles into account as well.

The flyers are also of significance because the birds stem from them. Indeed, a number of scientists believe that the early birds were so similar to some of the smaller dinosaurs that the two must have been directly related and that the birds are, in fact, the only surviving descendants of the dinosaurs.

There are three major groups of marine reptiles. They are the dolphinlike Ichthyosaurs, the Plesiosaurs and the Mosasaurs.

In this drawing of 1836, made just after the discovery of the Age of Reptiles, an Ichthyosaurus *devours a* Plesiosaurus *amid a scene of predatory carnage.*

No one knows how the Ichthyosaurs evolved. These sleek, finned reptiles bore little apparent relationship to any of the land-based forms described so far. Their bodies were superbly adapted to the marine environment, streamlined and tipped with a long pointed snout. Their limbs, though containing their full compliment of reptilian bones, were compressed and flattened into front and rear flippers. Many species had vicious sets of teeth and they must have lived by hunting fish, squid and cuttlefish.

The rear end of the backbone had a strange downward kink in it. At first this was thought to be the result of some disturbance of the skeleton after death and several species were mounted with the backbone straightened out. Later it was realized that the backbone kinked down to act as a strut for the lower part of the tail, which in later species looked identical to that of a dolphin. The evolution of this efficient means of propulsion can be clearly seen from the fossil record: the earliest Ichthyosaurs had a tail with only a small kink and which was formed with one dominant powerful fin. Later species showed an abrupt kink and a tail of two equal lobes.

Since they were so utterly adapted to life in water, Ichthyosaurs could not come out on to the land. They must therefore have given birth to their young alive, as dolphins do.

The Ichthyosaurs evolved during the Triassic and the early ones were contemporaries of creatures called Nothosaurs which looked like giant carnivorous newts, with tails that were flattened to act as paddles, and webbed feet. They must have been shallow water marine predators who returned to land to breed. Though rather primitive looking creatures, they were in fact extraordinarily successful and inhabited coastlines from Europe to Japan, lazing on rocks as seals do today.

Their probable descendants were the Plesiosaurs, which were fully aquatic, with large flippers and long reptilian necks. Plesiosaur means 'near-reptile', for it was once thought that they were animals in the throes of evolving from aquatic animals into reptiles. The largest ones measured between 40 and 50 feet long. They must have moved somewhat as turtles do now, rowing themselves along with their flattened limbs.

They were once referred to as swan-lizards but there was little of the swan about them. They could more aptly be described as turtles with snakes strung though them. The turtle image was unwittingly accurate; no young have been found inside Plesiosaur skeletons, suggesting the notion that they led a turtle-like existence, returning to the shores to lay eggs. If so, a Jurassic shore must have seen the heavy females laboring up the beach on their paddles to bury eggs that would have hatched safely a foot or two down, releasing young Plesiosaurs an inch or two long to scramble and tumble their way down to the sea.

Plesiosaurs, which have acquired some recent notoriety as suggested candidates to explain the Loch Ness Monster, evolved in one branch into short-necked versions known as Pliosaurs, which developed remarkably heavy heads and may have lived, as sperm whales do today, largely on cuttlefish. The Pliosaurs culminated in a monster of some note, *Kronosaurus*, whose 13-foot skull gave it the largest head of any reptile.

The Mosasaurs were the largest lizards ever, as well as being fully marine. They looked like Plesiosaurs who had been crossed with crocodiles. They probably used their long necks to seize passing fish, or even an unwary *Pteranodon*, drifting along a few inches clear of the surface in its search for small fry. They were in fact quite closely related to present-day monitor lizards, though the connection was disguised by the shape of the tail, which was flattened like an oar for swimming, and by their limbs, which were short paddles with webbed fingers and toes.

They were large—up to 50 feet, compared with the 10-12 feet of today's largest monitor, the Komodo dragon. Mosasaurs had huge jaws, the lower halves of which were jointed (like monitors' jaws) to allow them to separate at the hinge (as monitors' jaws do) to allow them to swallow massive chunks of food. They probably hunted almost anything that moved. They certainly crunched up ammonites, extinct squid-like creatures protected by a shell. One ammonite shell, punctured by Mosasaur teeth, showed evidence of such an encounter. The Mosasaur siezed its prey, bit into it several times, failed to

ABOVE: *The fossilized jaws of a Mosasaur, found near Maastricht, Holland in 1770. The jaws gave rise to the idea that there had once existed races of huge reptiles.* INSET: *Dr Hoffman supervises the removal of the fossil.* RIGHT: *An ammonite fossil showing teeth marks.*

swallow it, dropped it, picked it up again and this time succeeded in tearing out the soft parts, which it consumed, leaving the shell to sink to the ocean floor where it was fossilized.

No young Mosasaurs have ever been found, although adult fossils are common enough. It has been suggested that the females went up rivers to breed and that the young remained in fresh water until old enough to fend for themselves in the open sea.

None of these animals belonged to the Archosaurs, the group that includes the dinosaurs proper. Only one Archosaur species reconquered the sea. These were the sea-crocodiles, some of which grew to a fearsome 50 feet in length. They ate squid and octopus. Yet for some reason the sea-crocodiles did not make the grade. They did not survive even to the end of the Cretaceous.

The sea-going reptiles that did survive—and still exist—were the turtles. These seem immune to change, although the age of reptiles did throw up its usual record—*Archelon*, a turtle with a shell 10 feet long. They have remained pretty much the same for the past 200 million years—a permanent warning for those who would write off any creature as 'primitive'.

Besides conquering the land and reinvading the sea, the Archosaurs also took to the air. They did so in at least four different ways: as parachutists, as four-legged gliders, as winged reptiles—and finally as birds.

The first known flier was an early Triassic hummingbird-sized lizard called *Longisquama* ('long scale'). This tiny creature—which may, when its affinities are known, turn out to be the smallest Archosaur of all—had two banks of filmy scales coming out of its back that it

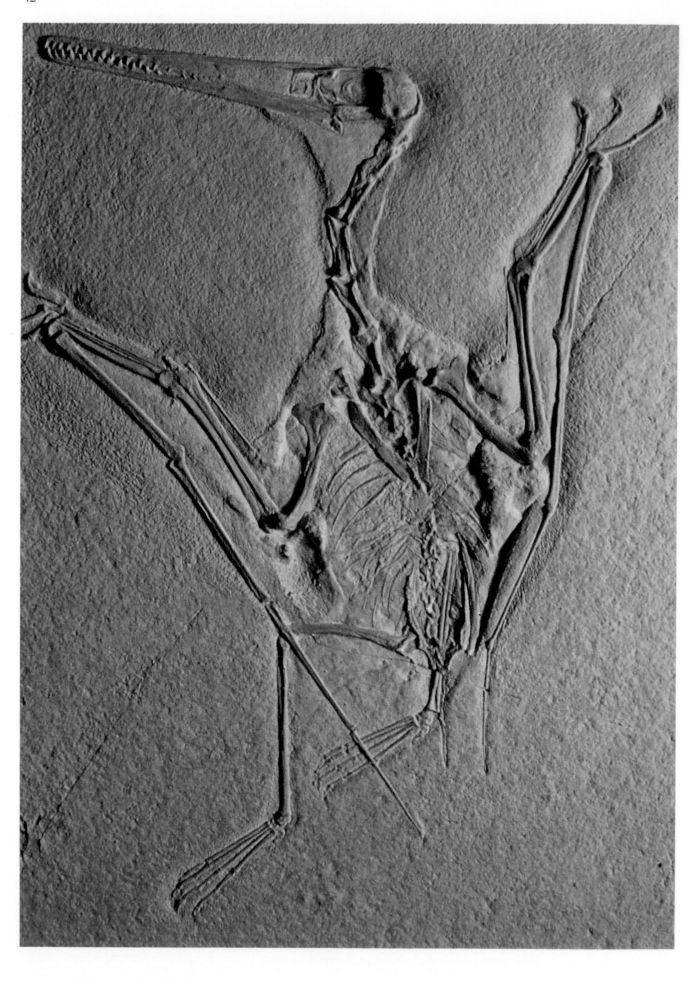

presumably spread out to either side to act as something between a wing and a parachute. If these were primitive wings, they were of a special sort, for they did not issue from the fore-limbs and therefore cannot count as the original version of the wings that later evolved on birds themselves.

The second early flier was the mouse-sized *Podopteryx* ('foot wing') which possessed flaps of skin between the fore and rear limbs, and between the rear limbs to the base of the tail. It must have looked something like a modern flying lizard. *Podopteryx* must have spread its membranes in a flash of color to glide from tree to tree.

Nor were these two types alone, even in Triassic times. There were gliding lizards which did evolve membranous extensions from their ribs. One of them is named, suitably enough, *Icarosaurus* after the mythical Greek who built himself prototype wings.

The relationship between these various creatures is obscure, but it seems likely that the *Podopteryx* was a predecessor of the later Pterosaurs, or 'flying lizards'. As Pterosaurs evolved, the leading membrane—that between the front and rear limbs—became increasingly important, until it became a proper wing, supported by the forearm, hand and a spindly fourth finger.

The first Pterosaur—or Pterodactyl ('winged finger') as Pterosaurs used to be known—ever

found was thought to be a ray-like fish or a cross between a bird and a bat. But it was concluded that its vertebrae and legs were those of a lizard and that it was definitely reptilian. It also had a long snout, toothed, with clawed fingers halfway along its wing.

Like birds, many species had short, broad wings that characterized flapping flight. They needed similar coordinating abilities, linked to an acute sense of vision. This meant that their brains were remarkably bird-like. Unlike a normal reptilian brain, a Pterosaur's brain completely filled its brain case. In some species the case—enlarged to accomodate the brain—was a dome of bone. The cerebellum at the back, which controls movement and balance and is not normally well developed in reptiles, is clearly of great importance to birds and Pterosaurs. The optic lobes of the mid-brain, which coordinate vision and were not normally well developed in dinosaurs, were huge in Pterosaurs and bear a striking resemblance to those of birds. It seems likely that to develop bird-like behavior, the pterosaurs had bird-like intelligence.

Their respiratory systems were probably bird-like as well. Powered flight demands a good deal of energy. Their muscles would have needed to be as efficient as those of birds. Perhaps their metabolism was comparable to that of birds in other ways as well. Birds breathe differently from mammals. They have no diaphragm, relying instead on the expansion and

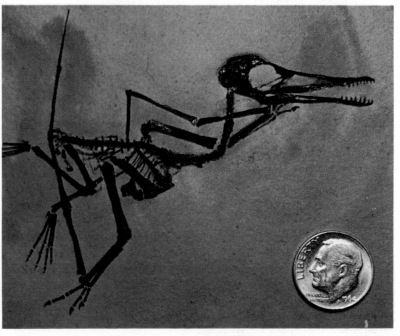

Although pterosaurs were usually restored as rather unappealing creatures, these two skeletons (left and right) from Solnhofen, West Germany reveal the beauty and delicacy of their structure. The claws and teeth that characterized them are clearly in evidence.

contraction of the muscles of the body wall to force air in and out. In addition, to supply the oxygen they need, they have air sacs that extend into their bones. Some species even have air sacs in their toes.

How birds actually make use of their air sacs is a matter of some conjecture but it is certain that the sacs assist in processing inhaled air and also help in cooling (birds do not sweat). Pterosaurs, like birds, possessed small openings into their hollow bones and their physiology may have been equally complex and equally efficient.

Given all this, why should they be classified as reptiles? Surely their high metabolism is completely non-reptilian. The Pterosaurs must have been intelligent, fast-moving and with high endurance, for they were presumably not rapidly grounded by exhaustion as a flying lizard would be. And they would surely have had a four-chambered heart to avoid reptilian circulation in which the oxygen-rich arterial blood is diluted with oxygen-deficient venous blood. The conclusion is that Pterosaurs might have been warm-blooded, like mammals and birds. Even if this idea becomes widely accepted, Pterosaurs are bound to be classed as reptiles for many years to come.

If these conclusions are true, Pterosaurs must have been insulated. All small creatures with a high metabolic rate—mammals and birds alike—need insulation. There are are no naked birds and very few small hairless mammals.

It has been argued that Pterosaurs were covered with fine hair. Bat skins have been compared to skin impressions of Pterosaurs and they were found very similar. In 1970 a small Pterosaur was found beautifully preserved in a lake deposit in the Soviet Union. The fine-grained rock showed delicate details like the wing membranes—and a furry pelt so clear that individual hairs could be seen. There was even hair on the fingers halfway along the front edge of the wing and on the membranes between the toes.

Pterosaurs were possibly bird-like in their reproductive behavior, too. They may well have laid eggs like their reptilian ancestors. Even if they brought forth their young alive, however, they would have needed to expend considerable care in feeding their offspring and keeping them warm. They must have paired, nested and lived in colonies—in fact, done many of the things that modern birds do.

There was one other characteristic of some Pterosaur species that made them remarkable: their size. *Pteranodon* measured 20 feet in wingspan. It had a long toothless beak balanced by an elongated bony crest jutting back from the top of the skull. It was found in marine sediments and was a coast-dweller. Its body was no longer than that of a turkey. It was really all wing.

It also had strange trailing hind limbs which would have made landing ungainly. It is hard to imagine how they ever could have landed. It has been suggested that they crash-landed on their bellies and then somehow shunted themselves along with their reversed hind limbs, supporting themselves on the clawed front limbs situated halfway along their wings. Once safely down, it was thought that *Pteranodon* could have used its back legs to hang in bat-like fashion from rocky ledges, dropping off to to ride the air currents out to sea, where it fed on fish.

The flight mechanisms of the *Pteranodon* were remarkable. At first it was not appreciated how amazing these mechanisms were. But *Pteranodon* was a flight engineer's dream. Every part of its skeleton was designed for a combination of lightness and strength to solve the aerodynamic problems posed by its size.

There has never been much question about the flying abilities of small Pterosaurs. But large ones faced considerable difficulties and the larger they were, the more severe were the problems. Birds face the same problems. As size increases, weight goes up even faster, for a large body needs broader wings, which demand a whole range of back-up systems—muscle, bones, heart, lungs, digestive tract. The effects are dramatic.

When size is doubled—assuming shape and structure remain in proportion—weight increases eightfold. Other factors, such as the strain on the wings and power requirements, increase in proportions that are similarly imposing. This means that the larger the flying crea-

ture, the more subtle its weightsaving engineering has to be. Theoretically, the interaction between these elements allows engineers to calculate an upper limit to Pterosaur size. Until recently, *Pteranodon* was thought to represent that limit.

In *Pteranodon* the reduction in weight seems to have been taken to its logical conclusion. Scaling up a bird in proportion puts *Pteranodon's* weight at some 200 pounds. In fact it weighed only 35 pounds because only 30 percent of its skeleton was solid; the rest was taken up with air sacs. Its wing bones, backbone and hind limbs were tubular, like aircraft struts. All of its bones were of eggshell delicacy —in some cases their walls were an unbelievable 1/25 of an inch thick, as was the membrane of its wings. It must have floated along as lightly as a kite.

Pteranodon is seen as the ultimate in gliding efficiency. It would hardly have needed to flap its wings at all. It took off by dropping away from its cliff nest to drift easily over the waves, whose updrafts supported it as it dipped its head for fish. Updrafts at cliff faces would take it back to its nesting place again.

Even the crest was seen as a marvelous adaptation to avoid extra muscle power. It needed a long beak to fish, but such a beak had

Although Pteranodons *were probably gull-like in their habits, it is unclear how they coped with their delicate, kite-like, 25-foot wingspan when landing on rocky surfaces.*

one disadvantage: if *Pteranodon* turned its head sideways, air pressure on the beak would have demanded powerful neck muscles to turn the head back to the forward position. The crest avoided the need for extra neck muscles —its large surface area acted as an automatic stabilizer. When the head was turned, the pressure on the beak was balanced by a corresponding pressure on the crest which brought the head into the forward position again. The crest weighed only an ounce or two, but to achieve the same effect with muscle would have demanded a half pound of flesh.

Pteranodon would have glided at about 15 mph and at that speed it would have been a better glider than any bird. Its wings locked into a gliding position with a special adaptation of the joint. But—and it is a big but— perhaps *Pteranodon* could never have had enough muscle to flap its wings.

To understand this requires in explanation of the dynamics of flapping flight. If the mass of a bird doubles, its wingspan must go up by a factor of three. This is fine for gliders but not for those creatures wishing to attempt powered flight. With increasing wingspan, the number of flaps per second falls and the power of the muscles—given the fact that they must all be tucked in near the body—must be more than squared. But as muscle power increases, the strain on the wing increases disproportionately. Heavier bones are required, which demand heavier muscles, which increase the bulk of the body, which again demands more wing area, and even heavier bones and more muscle.

All these effects react with each other and define an effective upper limit for powered flight. Icarus, the mythical Greek who built wings which collapsed in the heat of the sun, would never have got airborne. He would have needed a wingspan of 50 feet or so simply to glide, and to flap wings 50 feet across powerfully enough to lift a man's weight would demand muscles so massive that the span of the wings would actually need to be increased to several hundred feet. Clearly, no flying creature much larger than *Pteranodon* could exist.

On the other hand, there was a famous mathematical analysis of a bumblebee which proved conclusively that bees cannot fly. Nature is more ingenious than equations give credit for. Perhaps the above conclusion is a bit risky.

Wind tunnel tests have been done on model *Pteranodon* wings and it was concluded that these wings can be compared to the sails of a yacht. A yacht's sail, when tacking hard into the wind, adopts a shape that is not ideal for a glider, held taut as it is along the bottom edge by the boom. In the case of *Pteranodon* the 'booms' are represented by its body and back legs. The 'sail' (or wing) tends to billow upward and outward increasingly as it nears the tip. In a gliding creature like the *Pteranodon* this effect progressively altered the angle at which the membrane struck the air along the length of the wing. This meant that in gliding, lift also varied along the wing, decreasing gliding efficiency.

If *Pteranodon* could have flapped, however, it could have overcome this effect. In flapping flight, lift is achieved by the forward swing of the wings which pivot from the shoulder socket so that the tip moves faster through the air than the root. The airflow in flapping flight would counteract the effect of the distortion due to the 'yacht sail' effect. So *Pteranodon* might have been more efficient as a flapper, not a glider.

What then of the supposed upper limits in the weight of muscles? Musculature in birds varies between 15 and 35 percent of the animal's weight, and if *Pteranodon* were built in proportion it could not have flown at all. But bats' muscles comprise only 6 to percent of the total weight. Could we assume that *Pteranodon's* muscles were at least that efficient? Moreover, bats have a far greater variety of muscles to flap their wings. If we add the possibility that *Pteranodon* flew no more than 12 mph, take off from a stand still becomes possible with a wing-beat of one stroke per second. Perhaps, in addition, the wing was whippy at the tip, a flexibility seen both in bats and in pigeons which increases control and efficiency.

Perhaps the crest had an additional function: it may have acted as an anchor for a membrane that stretched down from the skull to the backbone to act as both a rudder and a means of controlling the head when the creature was fishing. With these lower requirements, *Pteranodon* could have generated 0.1 horsepower, but would have needed only 0.07 horsepower. In this analysis *Pteranodon* emerged not as a puzzling anomaly but as a creature of supreme efficiency—an animal of long flight endurance, a slow, but highly maneuverable flapping species.

The remains of a creature that dwarfed *Pteranodon* were found in Texas in 1975. *Quetzalcoatlus northropi* had a 17 1/2 inch armbone and it was calculated that it had a wingspan of about 50 feet—four times that of

ABOVE: *A* Pteranodon, *once thought to have been the largest flying creature ever.* LEFT: Archaeopteryx, *usually described as an ancestral bird, was a feathered dinosaur.*

the largest known flying bird, the wandering albatross.

It had apparently taken the weight-saving talents manifested by *Pteranodon* to even greater extremes. If it had been merely a scaled up *Pteranodon*, it would have weighed 290 pounds. In fact, the huge arm bone was so light that it felt like styrofoam. Although hollow, it was strengthened internally by minutely corrugated slats of bone to resist the lengthwise compression applied by the muscles on takeoff.

Indeed, it must have been able to take off. It was an inland dweller in an area where there were no mountains at the time. It could not have relied on cliffs to dive from. Nor could it have relied on regular breezes to lift it into the air. There was a huge bulge on the arm bone which was clearly an attachment for muscles, which equally clearly must have evolved to provide *Quetzalcoatlus* with powered flight.

How it did so without injury to its spindly structure will have to be figured out in the future. How, for instance, could it beat downward when standing, without hitting its wingtips on the ground? It is possible that its wings were flexible at their tips. When it took off, the area of wing near the body could have been enough to lift it well clear of the ground in its first flap. The wingtips, curled upward out of harm's way, could then have whipped down below the level of the body, providing an extra bit of lift. Once in the air it could have flapped slowly away with wave-like beats of its wings.

It must also have been able to glide extremely efficiently. This would have suited its supposed life style. Its neck bones suggest that it was a scavenger. The best preserved neck vertebrae, which are from smaller individuals, are up to 16 inches long. Since there were seven vertebrae in a Pterosaur's neck, even a conservative estimate would give the creature a reach of eight or nine feet. On this basis, it could have been a carrion-eater that used its snake-like neck to probe the carcasses of other dinosaurs.

There had also evolved from some primitive and highly disputed reptilian stock a flying creature of a completely different type: the bird. The birds are one of the most dramatic life forms ever to have appeared on earth. Their some 9000 species represent one of the five major divisions of vertebrates, along with mammals, reptiles, amphibians and fish. Their success must depend in large measure on the one thing that marks them as separate—their feathers. How feathers developed and when—and to which creatures birds are most closely related—has been a mystery since the first fossil bird was found in 1861.

The skeleton of this bird, called *Archaeopteryx lithographica* ('ancient wing from lithographic limestone') created a sensation. Here was a creature that was clearly a bird in that it possessed feathers. But it was also a reptile in that it had clawed fingers on its wings and a long bony tail. In 1877 another *Archaeopteryx* was found, and this specimen showed that the animal had teeth.

A comparison between *Archaeopteryx* and its small bipedal contemporary, *Compsognathus,*

one of the smallest dinosaurs known, reveals similarities. Both were pigeon-sized. Their limbs were very similar, although the *Archaeopteryx* had longer fore-limbs. Both had three fingers and four toes; both had bony tails; both had teeth and both had the abdominal ribs that characterize many dinosaurs.

But what about the feathers? Such extraordinary appendages must have demanded tens of millions of years of evolution. Until recently this was seen as a fundamental division. Bird was bird, and dinosaur was dinosaur. Whatever the similarities, it was widely accepted that any resemblance between *Archaeopteryx* and its dinosaur contemporary was coincidental. The differences were emphasized, the similarities played down. No modern bird has a tail containing vertebrae. Only one—the Amazonian hoatzin—has claws on its wings. *Archaeopteryx* possessed a bird-like wishbone unknown in dinosaurs. Moreover its hip structure was clearly bird-like and unlike the pelvis of *Compsognathus*.

But dinosaurs have been unearthed with clavicles or collarbones which may have fused together in the ancestors of birds to form wishbones. Perhaps the apparently backward pointing pubis may have been broken during fossilizing. In life, it could well have been down-turning like that of other carnivorous dinosaurs. *Archaeopteryx* could have been derived from an early, or mid-Jurassic dinosaur.

The significance of that theory is rather startling. Dinosaurs did not become extinct without descendants—their descendants are birds. This theory is far from being accepted, however.

It seems certain that birds have reptilian ancestors of some kind or other. How then to explain the feathers? The evolution of the wing has always been a puzzle. A wing, it was once assumed, was a device evolved for flight. But how could it evolve? Any creature that attempted flight with an 'evolving' wing would crash-dive to its death. If birds evolved to fly, how do we explain the necessarily instantaneous development of the wing?

One way out of this dilemma is to avoid the question and assume that feathers did not evolve for flight. They could have evolved for insulation. It is possible to see the ancestors of *Archaeopteryx* as fast-moving, small dinosaurs with a high metabolic rate, and therefore qualifying as hot-blooded adaptations to a colder climate, well insulated by early versions of feathers. Since these early birds could almost certainly climb trees, it requires no great leap of the imagination to see them as evolving an ability to parachute with their feathers as *Longisquama* had done. From there the evolutionary path is open to gliding flight and finally to powered flight which appeared as 'an evolutionary afterthought.'

The strongest argument that feathers were insulation comes from the near-certainty that *Archaeopteryx* could not have actually used them to fly. It lacked a solid breastbone, which provides the main attachment area for the wing muscles in flying birds and any solid crests on the upper arm to which flight muscles would have attached. The shoulder joint is typically dinosaurian: the socket points downward and the creature would have had difficulty raising its arms high enough to flap effectively.

Although slight in dinosaurian terms, it would have been heavily built for a bird and would have needed a tremendous bulk of muscle to get off the ground. Studies on the flying requirements of a bird the size of *Archaeopteryx* have shown that its bone might just have been strong enough to support it in gliding flight, but that to flap—even if it had the muscle—would have snapped its arm bones.

The argument for the warm-bloodedness of *Archaeopteryx* goes like this. Feathers insulate. Only a warm-blooded creature needs to be insulated. Therefore, warm-bloodedness had already developed in the ancestors of the *Archaeopteryx*. *Archaeopteryx* needed insulation. With feathers—like fur—a layer of air would be trapped next to the skin and act as a temperature buffer.

The need for insulation could explain much about the evolution of feathers. But it may not be a total explanation. The long wing feathers would not have provided much insulation. Nor would they have been of much use if *Archaeopteryx* had been mainly a tree-climber. On the contrary, they would have got in the way. Besides, they were not fixed to the bone and must have been loosely implanted in the flesh. They would not have provided any support in gliding or parachuting.

Being a running predator and needing to be well insulated, *Archaeopteryx* may have used its feathers as a net to surround and trap insects before grasping them with its claws. Perhaps it was this that demanded the high coordination necessary for flight.

The essential link between ground-dwelling predators and flyers is missing, but by the end of the Cretaceous there were 14 known genera of birds. It was only after the end of the dinosaurs, however, that the birds came into their own.

A painting that recreates how an Archaeopteryx *might have become fossilized—a clumsy flyer swept to its death by a high wind over a shallow sea. In fact,* Archaeopteryx *probably could not fly; its bones were too weak.*

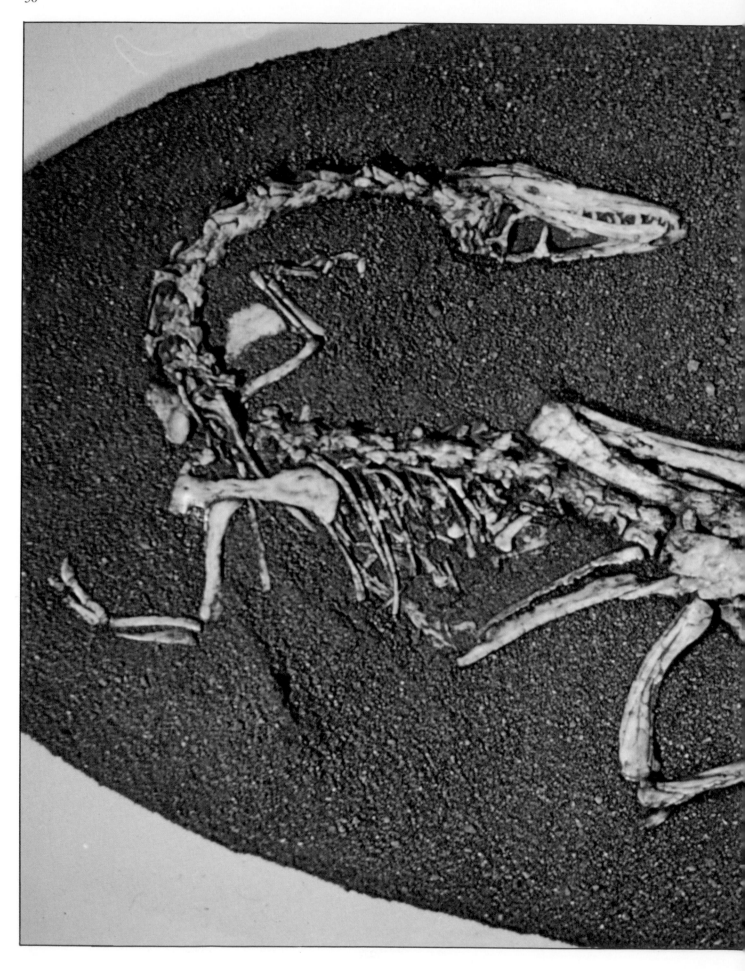

5 The Great Death

Sixty-five million years ago, the dinosaurs vanished. This event, which marks the end of the Cretaceous period, must rank as one of the most startling occurrences in the history of life on earth. After 140 million years of steadily increasing success, the dinosaurs—and many hundreds of other contemporary species on the land, in the air, and in the sea—disappeared from the face of the earth. One stratum reveals in its fossil record a wide diversity of creatures, another stratum, just a few million years younger, contains by comparison a mere handful.

The problem seems a simple one: what force could have brought about such a catastrophe? When posed this way—with the assumption of a rapid catastrophic extermination—the question seems to demand a simple explanation. And explanations there have been in plenty, most of them dramatically straightforward and some of them laughably bizarre. Before we look at the question in depth, consider this checklist of suggested explanations for the death of the dinosaurs.

• Climatic change: the world, warm and muggy for so long, began to dry out and get even hotter so that the dinosaurs got roasted

A distorted fossilized Coelophysis *skeleton.*

out of existence. Alternatively the climate became colder and they froze to death.

• They became so successful that they ate up all their food and died of starvation.

• Their food became poisoned.

• They were killed by disease or newly evolving parasites.

• The dinosaurs became so heavy that their bodies simply refused to work. They slipped their discs too frequently to survive.

• The atmosphere changed. Volcanoes, meteorites or comets poisoned the earth.

• The dinosaur eggs were all stolen by agile, nimble and intelligent mammals.

• The dinosaurs died of 'racial old age'—a concept suggesting that species can be treated as individuals and that after a time they simply succumb to senility.

• The carnivorous dinosaurs ate all the herbivorous dinosaurs and then died of hunger themselves.

• A star exploded nearby in the galaxy and doused the earth in a lethal dose of radiation.

• The gravity of a passing star pulled the earth in two, thus creating the moon. The resulting catastrophic earthquakes and tidal waves wiped out the dinosaurs.

• Geological changes brought droughts and floods with which the dinosaurs could not cope.

• They could not stand to live any more and died of depression.

• They could not cope with the chemistry of the newly-evolved flowering plants and died of constipation.

• Newly-evolved insects, living off the flow-

ering plants, ate them out of existence.

However much fun these suggestions are, they do not help us to understand the extinction. The inadequacies of most of these explanations become clear if the problem is restated in terms that conform a little more to the known facts. It is then possible to ask what patterns can be devised to fit the findings. Only then can the right answers be found.

What exactly did vanish at the end of the Cretaceous? The dinosaurs themselves went —several hundred species in all. Many other reptilian forms also vanished with them: Pterosaurs—including, of course, the last of the flying giants, the *Quetzalcoatlus*—Ichthyosaurs, Plesiosaurs and Mosasaurs. Toothed birds became extinct. So too did ammonites (shelled molluscs that were coiled into flat spirals rather like a modern nautilus), many groups of sea-snails and other whole groups of squid-like and cuttlefish— like creatures called belemnites.

But one of the most telling features about the so-called Cretaceous-Tertiary boundary— besides the disappearance of the dinosaurs—is the change of microscopic life forms in the sea. Of course, the most significant for our purposes are the foraminifera—tiny shelled creatures that range in size from the microscopic up to about two inches across.

They are an important constituent in plankton, those minute life-forms, both plant and animal, that drift by the countless billions in the sea, turning it into an organic soup on which almost all marine life is ultimately dependent. From the surface, the minute shells of the hundreds of species of foraminifera rain down continuously on the bottom, where they form a major part of the so-called 'globigerina ooze' which covers about 30 percent of the ocean floor.

Their fossil record is extraordinary. Their shells—or tests—are found in marine strata over two-thirds of the world's existing land areas and they thus serve as a good indication of the extent of ancient seas. There is for instance, a 200-foot stratum of foraminifera at the 22,000-foot level on Mount Everest. During the Cretaceous, when the sea level was high,

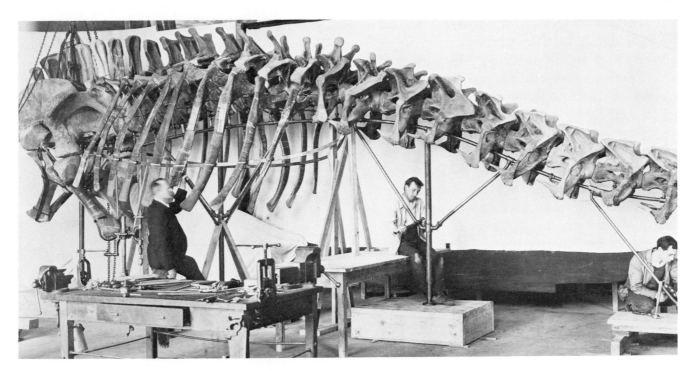

ABOVE: The brontosaur, unearthed between 1909 and 1922, was given the scientific name of Apatosaurus louisiae. *This shot was taken during the reconstruction work.*

foraminifera were widely distributed across North America and Europe. The White Cliffs of Dover were laid down at that time.

At the end of the Cretaceous, countless existing species of foraminifera vanished from the fossil record to be replaced by species of a totally different type. Many of the Cretaceous species were unusually large, yet those that marked the beginning of the Tertiary were singularly small. On this evidence it was concluded that at the end of the Cretaceous there was a major regression of the sea and a drastic cooling of the oceans. The death of the dinosaurs coincided with the onset of the colder climate.

The evidence for such a change is strong, too, from the fossil record of pollen grains, which are the toughest part of flowering plants and leave a record in the rock of the plant life of each period. In eastern Montana, fossil pollen reveals that half of all late Cretaceous plants were flowering plants. Early in the Tertiary the proportion had dropped to less than one-third, and the conifers, which tolerate colder conditions, had increased their hold.

How long did such changes take? The destruction of foraminifera could have been very rapid. Estimates have varied form a few days to a million years. Trees, of course, spread relatively slowly. It would take several hundred generations for a forest community to be replaced in a changing climate.

The fossil record of the dinosaurs also indicates that their end was not immediate. In a Cretaceous bed in the western part of the United States, 16 genera of horned dinosaurs have been found, while in the last stratum there were only seven genera represented. The armored dinosaurs show a similar reduction, from 19 to six genera, and the duck-billed forms from 29 to seven. In this perspective the final extinction at the end of the Cretaceous should be seen as the culmination of a steady process that went on over a period of several million years.

What survived the change? Firstly the mammals, which were already beginning to diversify. At the end of the Cretaceous, the largest mammals, already divided into placentals (whose young are born at an advanced stage of development) and marsupials (whose young are raised in pouches) were probably the size of a cat. The birds survived, and then, after the extinction of the dinosaurs, exploded into a wide variety of types. The fish came through largely unscathed. But most puzzling of all, a few reptilian types also survived—turtles, crocodiles, lizards, snakes (which had evolved only a short time before) and the peculiar tuatara of New Zealand, the sole surviving member of an obscure and pre-dinosaurian group of reptiles.

There are two other factors that should be emphasized: throughout the Cretaceous, sea-levels were high, as the evidence of foraminifera deposits shows. Huge deposits of chalk were laid down by seas that spread across Central Europe, North Africa and the midwest section of the United States. But at the end of the Cretaceous, the seas retreated, exposing areas that had been previously covered. Secondly, by the end of the Cretaceous, the continents were almost completely split up. Eurasia, Africa, India, Antarctica (still joined to Australia and the Americas) were all separate continental islands.

What patterns can be imposed on these facts that make sense?

Let us look first at some of the more widely discussed theories in detail and examine the objections to them: almost all of them are either too limited, in that they should really apply only to individual species, or too general, in that they do not account for the selectivity of the great death.

Take, for instance, the suggestion that disease was responsible for the extinction of the dinosaurs. There are indeed virulent diseases that have swept through animal and human populations—rabies, rinderpest, anthrax, myxomatosis, the Black Death. There are two remarkable things about such plagues. One is that they do not in fact wipe out complete species, however virulent they are. A small percentage of individuals—either through immunity or luck—escapes to rebuild the population.

Myxomatosis was introduced into Australia to control the plague of rabbits; but although the disease can wipe out 90 percent of a population in a fairly short time, it is remarkable how little lasting impact such a catastrophe has. Within a few years—a mere eye-blink of geological time which would never be recorded in the fossil record—the population balance was restored. In Australia, myxomatosis is now only 30 percent fatal and the more normal limits imposed by food supply and natural predators prevail once again.

Such is the case with other equivalent catastrophes. Lemmings, driven every few years to run themselves into the sea in a frantic search for food, rebuild their depleted populations rapidly.

Secondly, very few plagues affect several species equally. Bubonic plague killed one-third of the human population of Europe in the 14th century but it had no impact at all on the rats that carried the fleas that carried the disease. There are diseases that affect closely related species, but no disease is known that could affect a whole class—all mammals or all birds—simultaneously.

Plesiosaurs had the head, neck, body and flippers that are similar to descriptions given of the Loch Ness Monster.

creatures could grow old, just as individuals grew old, until they finally expired of old age. Evidence of senility was seen in the apparent 'extremes' of later dinosaurian evolution—the odd bony frills of *Triceratops*, the plumes of some duck-billed dinosaurs, the thick skulls of the dome-headed dinosaurs.

The argument, although initially appealing, does not withstand analysis. Since nothing physical passes from one generation into the next—genetic information is duplicated afresh—what exactly would 'age'? Would such aging apply to one species—in which case, is one to assume that a variety of species became old simultaneously by pure coincidence? Or does aging apply to groups of related species? Either way, why should some species apparently survive unscathed for many millions of years when other species succumb after a shorter life span?

Finally—and most conclusively—why should a species, or a group of species, be treated as an individual entity? Species evolve continuously, with varieties leading to new species. Often they do not die out at all: they change into something else.

Such philosophical problems in the theory led back to the supposed evidence for racial old age: the 'extremes' of adaptation displayed by late Cretaceous dinosaurs. A second look at these 'extremes' shows that the evidence for senility lies in the mind of the observer, not in the creatures themselves. Even the most bizarre adaptations evolved for a particular purpose and are there because they conferred some benefit on an individual, which survived at least long enough to breed.

Far from indicating senility, the range of adaptations in the later dinosaurs seems to display an increasing, not a decreasing, evolutionary vigor. They filled places in the food chain now occupied by lions, ostriches, elephants, buffalo and crocodiles. Among the last dinosaurs were some of the most impressive. Duck-billed dinosaurs could have had senses as delicate as our own—stereoscopic vision, an opposable thumb and extraordinary coordination.

The wide variety of dinosaurs suggests a possible science-fiction scenario: if the history of the earth had turned out differently, the

Moreover, even if there were such a disease, why would it leave some of the group of creatures completely unharmed? And why should the disease spread to the seas? And how, given the position of the continents, could such disease have spread from one continental landmass to another?

One once-popular idea was that of racial senility. It was claimed that whole races of

Cretaceous might have been the beginning of a great new dinosaurian evolutionary chapter rather than the end of one. What might not have evolved from such creatures, which had some of the characterisitics of the apes and monkeys that emerged some 40 million years later? Perhaps in some different dimension of time, we can imagine intelligent dinosaurs, with another 65 million years of evolution behind them, observing the fossil record and wondering why those tiny furry creatures, the mammals, never evolved into species of any significance.

In the search for causes to explain dinosaur extinction, scientists have naturally concentrated on those elements in the late Cretaceous that were new and to which the dinosaurs might not have been able to adapt. One such novelty was the emergence of the flowering plants which came into existence about 120 million years ago. it has been seen as significant that the extinction of the dinosaurs followed.

Non-flowering plant-like ferns and conifers contain tannins with which the herbivorous dinosaurs had coped well enough for tens of millions of years. The flowering plants contained a new sort of substance, the alkaloids, most of which produce harmful physiological changes in men and animals. Examples of alkaloids are morphine, quinine, nicotine and strychnine. Almost a thousand alkaloids are known, most of them restricted to particular groups of plants and most toxic to some degree, although about 20 are used in carefully controlled amounts for medicinal purposes. The effects are usually remarkably specific—raising blood pressure, stimulating the respiratory system, affecting the mind and behavior, producing paralysis.

Perhaps reptiles were less aware of such poisons than mammals. For example, tortoises eat 40 times as much of an alkaloid plant than mammals before becoming sensitized and cutting down their intake. since both tortoises and dinosaurs are reptiles, the dinosaurs might have been unable to detect alkaloids in low enough concentration to be harmless and may well have eaten enough to suffer severe physiological disturbance and even death. The implication is that once the herbivores vanished, the carnivores followed suit.

This is a nice idea, but it raises difficulties. In the first place it is unfair to compare tortoises with dinosaurs, whose physiology was possibly more equivalent to modern mammals than modern reptiles. Again there is the problem of selectivity: fish-eating Pterosaurs and Plesiosaurs should not have been affected, but they were. Turtles and tortoises should have been affected, but they weren't.

The most serious objection, however, is one of chronology: the dinosaurs survived for some 50 million years after the emergence of the flowering plants. It looks strongly as if the argument should be reversed and that it was the development of the flowering plants that allowed the dinosaurs to diversify in the way that they did. The bird-hipped dinosaurs, which had only a moderate success in jurassic times, increased five-fold in the late Cretaceous times. Two new large groups—the armored and the horned types—evolved. The duck-bills produced whole batteries of teeth to cope with the new source of food.

One argument that might seem to support death by poisoning is the peculiar distorted pose in which some skeletons have been found. A number of those with long necks have, in death or fossilization, been contorted so that the neck seems to have been thrown over the back. One explanation for these contortions is that they were the result of death throes brought on by strychnine poisoning, which does indeed induce muscular spasms before death. However, such distortions are not limited to dinosaurs, nor are they limited to the Cretaceous; it seems likely that the dessication of the neck tendons immediately after death caused the contortion before fossilization occurred.

Another theory is that the dinosaurs were eaten out of house and home by the arrival of the butterflies and moths, with their voracious plant-eating larvae—the caterpillars. It was the caterpillars, it has been suggested, that defoliated the world, hence depriving the herbivores of their food and consequently starving the carnivores as well. One almost insuperable obstacle to this theory is that the oldest known caterpillar fossils are from the Tertiary, long after the extinction of the dinosaurs.

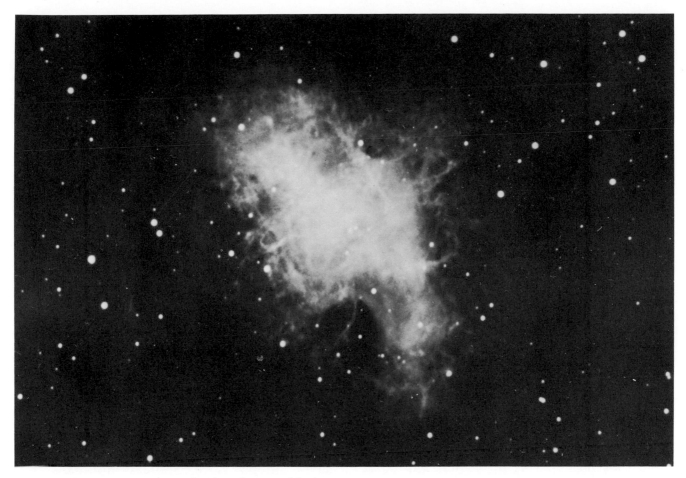

This fast-expanding cloud of gas is the remnant of a supernova—the Crab Nebula—which appeared in 1054 AD. A supernova has been suggested as the cause of the Great Death.

But let us suppose—the fossil record being incomplete—that there were caterpillars in the Cretaceous. Caterpillars nowadays are controlled by the birds which feed upon them. It is pretty certain that had a new food source like caterpillars evolved, the birds themselves would have evolved rapidly to take advantage of them. Moreover, if there were too few birds, why did not the dinosaurs themselves develop a liking for caterpillars?

Perhaps the most startling and one of the most compelling of the suggested explanations is that of a cosmic catastrophe—the type of event that would rival, in drama, the great extinction. One such catastrophe might have been a stellar explosion—a nova of supernova—occurring close enough to the earth to shower it with lethal cosmic radiation.

A nova ('new star') is a star that has exploded (a fate that may be a normal part of the evolution of all stars). A nova outburst may be from a hundred times to a million times brighter than the original star and the change characteristically takes place in just a few days. A supernova is an explosion that reaches many times that brightness. The total energy emitted by a nova may equal the rediation from the sun over 10,000 years but the total radiation emitted in a few days by a supernova may equal the energy radiated by the sun during 1000 million years.

Seen from the earth, one supernova in a distant galaxy—one star in perhaps 100 million—may outshine all its neighbors. On the average there is about one supernova per galaxy every 300 years. There have been five in our Milky Way during the last 1000 years, most notable, perhaps, the one observed by Chinese astronomers in 1054. The remnant of this explosion, known as the Crab Nebula, is a cloud of gas expanding at the rate of several hundred miles per second.

It is likely that several times in its history the earth has been bombarded by radiation from a nearby supernova, one that is within about 20 light years of the earth. It has been estimated that a local supernova in our own galaxy will occur once in a hundred million years. When this happens, the radiation level at the top of the atmosphere would shoot up about 100,000-fold. The effects of such an explosion on life on earth would probably be catastrophic.

In particular, the radiation would, but a rapid chemical process, destroy the ozone layer, which mops up almost all of the harmful short-wave radiation from the sun. Such destruction of the ozone layer would expose the earth's surface to the sun's lethal ultraviolet rays. Cosmic ray intensity might increase 100-fold and, since about one-third of the radioactivity of the earth's suface is the result of cosmic radiation, radioactivity would increase 30 times.

If such an event were to occur now, we might expect a dramatic rise in skin cancer, an increase in the mutation rate and extreme climatic changes, though whether we would fry or freeze is open to some dispute. If a local supernova occurred at the end of the Cretaceous, the dinosaurs would—according to this argument—have been subjected to rapid unendurable assaults on their bodies and habitats.

There are a number of objections to this dramatic and appealing theory. They relate to the two suggested effects: an increase in radiation and a change of climate.

To suggest radiation as the agency of destruction again involves the problem of selectivity. Given the similarity between the small fast dinosaurs and birds, why shuld one have been exterminated and the other survive? In addition, given the fact that a few inches of water can cut radiation even at that high level to practically nothing, how is it that some large marine creatures of reptilian origin vanished, while the fish remained unaffected? It is possible to assume that mammals, being small, might have burrowed out of the way of intense solar radiation, but it is a litttle hard to accept that all Cretaceous species were burrowers and that all would have remained underground for the several days or weeks that it took to deliver a lethal dose of radiation.

But a supernova also might have climatic effects. A heavy dose of radiation in the upper atmospheric layers would draw lower, moister air upwards, where it would form ice crystals that would reflect the sun's rays, causing a dramatic drop in temperature all over the world. It might have been the cold and not the radiation that caused the extinctins.

Yet this theory, too, suggests an instant catastrophe, a fact that is in conflict with the progessive diminution of dinosaur fossils through the strata of the late Cretaceous period. Nevertheless, the suggestion of a colder climate extended over a long period of time is worth examining. Suppose we simply postulate a colder climate without at first seeking an explanation. Could a new ice age have spelled the end of the dinosaurs?

Perhaps the dinosaurs emerged into an equitable and warm climate at the end of the Triassic. They had an efficient body chemistry that was comparable to that of a mammal and they certainly had no problem in dissipating the heat that they generated. What the dinosaurs did not have, and did not need, was insulation. They did not have to evolve adaptations to keep warm; their high metabolism and huge bulk, in combination with a warm climate, were sufficient to ensure a stable high temperature.

Although the Pterodactyls, lacking bulk, developed a furry covering, the dinosaurs themselves were naked. In a uniform, world-wide cold snap, they would have had no way to preserve their heat. True, the larger adults could have done so over a period of perhaps several weeks because their immense size preserved heat, but their offspring and the smaller species would have frozen as easily as plucked chickens in a freezer.

On the other hand there is no evidence for a uniform cold snap over the whole world. There was still an equator. Tropical forests diminished but they did not disappear. The Cretaceous rain forests of Borneo and the Amazon were very like today's rain forests. Although the dinosaurs might have been exterminated in many regions by cold, there is no apparent reason why they should not have survived in isolated pockets. After all, there are many relict communities of creatures scattered about the world, suvivors from a former age, whose niche has remained relatively untouched. Why did no herbivores survive on the edges of the Amazon Basin, along with the carnivores that preyed upon them? Why should the crocodiles, which are even more sluggish and, apparently, more susceptible to cold, survive? Climate, which certainly would have played some part in the great death, is not in itself a sufficient explanation.

There is, however, the beginning of an answer. Assume that we should not be looking for new and dramatic explanations for the Cretaceous exinction. Extinctions are as much a pattern of life as the evolution of a new species. The two processes go hand in hand, and any change—of which there have been many in the history of the earth—brings about a concentration of extinctions that may look dramatic in the fossil record but, in fact, merely reflect an intensification of the natural order of events.

In the great death at the end of the Cretaceous the really striking thing is not the type of creature that was eradicated, but its size. Generally anything over about 22 pounds vanished. Anthing weighing less than that survived. These weight limits happen to exclude all the mammals and include all the dinosaurs. Had there been a mammal of 22 pounds or more, it too would have vanished. Those reptiles that survived were all under 22 pounds, with the exception of crocodiles and turtles, which form a special case.

The fossil remains of a trilobite, a type of extinct Paleozoic marine animal whose body segments were divided by furrows on the top surface into three lobes.

But animals live in environments. Perhaps we should rephrase the question by asking not why the dinosaurs vanished but why their habitats vanished. And as an extension of this point, extinctions can be seen in two ways. One may ask, 'Why did the creatures die out?' which is the usual way of looking at the problem; or—since extinctions are as much a feature of life as the evolution of new species —one can rephrase the question and ask; 'Why did no new species emerge to replace those that would have gone extinct anyway?' To answer this, the most fruitful approach is to seek patterns underlying all extinctions.

In looking at the patterns of extinction from Permian times right through to the end of the Cretaceous, the death of the dinosaurs seems somewhat less dramatic. There are several 'extinction events' in the 200 or so million years from the end of the Permian to the end of the Cretaceous. During much of that time, the world was a single landmass.

Even right at the end of the Cretaceous there were still narrow land bridges between some of the major continental areas and the dinosaurian communities do not show the extraordinary variety that is exhibited by life-forms in the world today. The differences are of quantity rather than quality. For instance, South America had few duck-bills but many plant-eaters, while western North America had many horned dinosaurs and very few plant-eaters.

Most fossils are found on the flood-plain areas on the edges of continental landmasses. But these habitats are limited. They do not reflect the variety of species that actually existed on the continent at any one time. Nor do they act as a major evolutionary stimulus for the emergence of new species. Species develop in the continental interiors, where the variety of habitats—plains, forests, rivers, mountains, deserts—provides a wider variety of possible living places. They also form the large natural barriers that keep new varieties of old species separated until they have evolved enough to count as a new species.

From the interior, new species filter down into the lowlands. Assuming therefore that most of the animals that appear in the fossil record evolved in the continental interior, the question we should ask in order to seek an explanation of the great death is, 'Why did species stop evolving in the continental interiors?'

In all communities in the geological past there is a pattern. They begin with a low diversity of species, particularly of the larger herbivores. Diversity steadily increases, with a consequent increase in the number of carnivores, and then drops away again. In the Triassic, for instance, there were four major families of herbivores, which diminished at the beginning of the Jurassic. At the end of the Jurassic there were nine herbivore families.

Fully aquatic marine reptiles show a similar pattern. Diversity apparently increases as time goes on, as long as the environment provides the opportunities. Environments that remain unchanged—like fresh-water wetlands—do not show an increase in diversity. Crocodiles and turtles never evolved a wide variety of species. So what happened to the environment to limit diversity, particularly at the end of the Cretaceous?

In a unified landmass, climatic change is simply not enough to explain these extinctions. There is always a change of some kind going on, and if any stratum is analyzed closely enough, some evidence will be found for it, since such changes are part of the reason for the existence of separate strata. Sometimes this may produce local variations in the balance between the species or families, but even at the end of the Cretaceous when the climate was cooling down, the winters were still mild enough for crocodile-types to survive as far north as Saskatchewan. At any rate, extinctions occurred in the hot, dry continental interiors, such as Mongolia, as well as in the wet interior of Central North America.

About the only thing that does correlate well with the overall pattern of extinction is the sea level. Major drops in the sea level—regressions, as they are known—occurred between the Triassic and the Jurassic, between the Jurassic and Cretaceous and at the end of the Cretaceous. Since water acts as a buffer against large changes of temperature, such regressions would go hand in hand with lower temperatures. But as we have seen, this in itself is not enough to explain extinctions. What other effects could have been associated with the regressions?

First let us look at the machinery of speciation. Species evolve more quickly where there are wide variey of niches to accommodate them, and a variety of niches is associated with the more complex habitats of continental interiors. Natural barriers of any kind tend to increase speciation. These barriers may be extremely subtle and need not be geographical —a particular food source is good enough, such as that which interrelates eucalyptus trees and koalas—but often the barriers are large ones such as mountains and seas.

These are associated with high sea levels, or transgressions. Large scale transgression, therefore, is a form of evolutionary pressure and should result in the formation of new species. We should look for an explanation as to why no new species arose to replace those dinosaurian species that became extinct at the end of the Cretaceous.

The correlation between regressions and extinctions suggests the solution to two of the minor problems: the survival of fresh water aquatic species and the death of the large marine reptiles. Retreating seas do not affect the number of lakes and rivers. Higher lakes may dry up but lower ones are created, and rivers will always run down to the sea, however far away the sea is. Fresh water aquatic species, such as crocodiles and turtles, will simply migrate with their habitats and remain unaffected by any of the extinctions.

Secondly, the regression of the seas toward the edge of the continental shelves, where the coastlines plunge into the oceanic depths, means that there are fewer shallow seas. This would impose a pressure on any species that could not adapt itself to deep-sea living. Such may well have been the case with the Plesiosaurs. Mosasaurs and sea-crocodiles could have been similarly affected. The Ichthyosaurs had vanished earlier in the Cretaceous for reasons that are simply not known.

There is one problem: why should not a few species remain to fill the few remaining niches? What killed the last few species of dinosaurs? Perhaps the extinction was caused by one of the agents traditionally mentioned as the one and only reason for the extinction of all dinosaurs—climatic change, floral change, parasites or a combination of all these. Possibly the most likely of these was the increasing cold. If, at this stage, the engine of evolution had been still highly tuned, no doubt dinosaurian species would have evolved that could have coped with the increasing cold. Indeed, perhaps they already had appeared. They were the birds, who had evolved their insulation in the form of feathers.

This, of course, is not a total answer. There are a number of vital questions that still demand total and detailed consideration. Does the sea level, in fact, drop solely because the movement of the continents slows? Do species, in fact, evolve in the continental interiors? And why did the last surviving families die out, if there were still odd pockets in which they might have survived?

Nevertheless, if we try to relate geology and biology to other extinctions, it will surely stimulate others to criticize, theorize, seek new evidence and eventually perhaps to propose a watertight explanation of this fascinating problem.

With the disappearance of the dinosaurs the world was left with no large animals. There were no creatures to graze the grasslands or browse on the bushes, let alone the treetops. Hundreds of niches—even in an impoverished world—existed to be exploited, and there, lurking in burrows, scurrying between the roots of trees and clinging to the branches in the upper levels of the forests were the creatures who would now inherit the earth—the mammals.

Benjamin Waterhouse Hawkins, the man who created the London reconstructions of the Crystal Palace dinosaurs, sketched another display to be built in New York's Central Park. Unfortunately, it was never built.

INDEX

Acknowledgments

The author and publisher would like to thank the following
people who have helped in the preparation of this book: Anistatia
Vassilopoulos, who designed it; Thomas G. Aylesworth, who
edited it; Cynthia Klein, who prepared the index.

Credits

Artists
Richard Bell 2–3, 54
Linda Broad: 6–7, 9, 14, 15, 18 (below), 82 (bottom), 23 (below),
25, 31, 47
Petula Stone: 23 (above)

Photographs
Animals Unlimited Picture Library, Christina Payne/Paddy Cutts,
kindly provided all of the photographs used in this book.
Courtesy of the American Museum of Natural History: 53, 64
Dr Donald Baird: 12, 19 (top and center), 30, 34, 35, 41 (below),
42, 43, 50–51, 59
By Courtesy of the British Museum (Natural History): 29, 45
Michael Freeman: 26–27
Hayle Observatories: 57
Illustrated London News: 33, 36–37, 49
Patrimonie de l'Institut Royal des Sciences Naturelles de Belgique:
16, 17
Institut und Museum für Geologie und Paläontologie der
Universität, Tübingen, Photo: Werner Wetzel: 18 (above)
Mark Mason: Pronda Pronda (with thanks to the Oxford Museum):
142–143
By courtesy of the Museum für Naturkunde der Humboldt-
Universität, DDR Berlin: 4, 20–21
Musée Nationale d'Histoire Naturelle, Institut de Paléontologie,
Paris: 41 (above and inset)
Smithsonian Institution: Book cover, 2–3
© Walt Disney Productions: 8